Good luck !

and
giselle

714 435-4640

Networking...
The Natural
Extension
of You

Networking...
The Natural Extension
of You

By
John and Giselle Sexsmith
&
Boyd Matheson

Published by:
Innovative Learning Technologies, Inc.
8184 Highland Dr., Suite C-5
Sandy, Utah 84093
1-800-934-8946

ISBN 1-882441-51-6: $19.95 Hard Cover

Dedication

To our children who teach us to see life as it is; We love you.

To our friends; your lessons were never lost on us.

To the people and leaders at the home office; Thank you for not changing the finish line.

To the Networkers; You have not only had the dream but the determination to make them reality!

Table of Contents

Prologue

Why is it that some people continually produce incredible results in their lives while others with the same talents, abilities and opportunities don't? Is it luck, good genes, personal connections, education or just the stars? Have you ever thought that successful people are different or have an unfair advantage over you? If you have, you are not alone. The truth is that there is a peak performer in all of us. This book illustrates how two deeply committed individuals with no special training or contacts, rose to the pinnacles of success and achievement. They have personally destroyed many of the myths about what it takes to enjoy success and personal freedom.

John Sexsmith, a Canadian with a twelfth grade education and Giselle Sexsmith, a Puerto Rican accountant, married and created a dream life that exceeds the bounds of even the tallest of fairy tales. How did they do it? **Networking!**

A single idea from this book can change your life forever. Early on in the process of building a networking business, a time when they were being told by everyone that they couldn't succeed, John and Giselle were invited to go to their company's convention. John was not willing to go for any reason. He was not outgoing, didn't drink, and didn't want to golf or sit through meetings. Giselle was persistent and continued pressing John to go. Finally she got him to talk to one of the company executives. John asked for one good reason why he should spend his time and money to go to the convention. The Executive, without hesitation, replied that just one idea from the convention could put an additional $100,000 in his pocket over the next 12 months. That was reason enough for John, and it should be reason enough for you! Within the pages of this book are many ideas, principles and concepts that can put thousands of additional dollars into your purse or pocket. Put them to the test!

Are you frustrated and stressed out with your life and your present opportunities? How do you feel about your M.O.P.S. – Money, Occupational limitations, Physical restraints (lack of freedom to go and do what you want when you want) and Stress? If you have anxiety over any of these areas in your life, <u>this book is for you.</u> If you DON'T have any anxiety in these areas, <u>this book is for you</u>, too. John and Giselle's stimulating stories, personal experiences and application of success principles will bring you a better way of life. If you are already enjoying success, personally meeting Giselle and John within the pages of this book will take you to higher levels of satisfaction and freedom.

Perhaps the most difficult choice you make in your life is how you trade your time for money. It is also called "having a job." Frustration develops as you realize that you can't trade your time for money enough times to give yourself the life you want to live! The key is to extend yourself and train others to perform as well as you perform. Once you duplicate yourself, you will reap a grand harvest for your investment in others. When you build others, you build yourself. This is the magic of networking. This is the magic of "Having a Life!"

Networking... The Natural Extension of You! was written to help you create success through self -understanding. In order to succeed you have to teach yourself to be you! John and Giselle never intended to become leaders; they only wanted to live their values and make a contribution. Through the magic of networking they were able to discover themselves and become the best individuals they could be. Your challenge is to build and discover a better you and networking will help you do it.

As you embark on a new journey of self-discovery, you will look at your interactions with others and how you can multiply your effectiveness by giving all that you have and are to every one you meet. Creating "strategic alliances" will move you to the highest of heights and allow you to create a rewarding network of leaders and producers. There are no free lunches, but if you invest in yourself and strive to make the principles in this book a part of who you are, the natural by-product will be increased wealth, more quality and quantity time with your family, and the freedom to enjoy all that life has to offer. Be open to the ideas John and Giselle share with you. Remember, that "If you think the way you've always thought, you will continue to get what you've always got." This book will not make you a dime in and of itself, but if you use the principles and philosophies it contains and actively implement them, you will see truly amazing results. Incidentally, John went to the convention, and the gold mine of ideas and principles did indeed put an extra $100,000 in his pocket over the following 12 months.

John and Giselle understand achievement and success because they have lived and continue to live the dream each day. As you internalize these principles and start to achieve, you will come to fully understand that success is a thousand times better than you ever imagined it could be. You will enjoy this success even more because you will fully become you. You will understand who you really are and what you can become. Creating achievement in networking is like turning on the color in a black and white world. As a result of your network your life will become more vivid, alive, and vibrant and you will experience all the colors of the rainbow and all that the world has to offer. Begin your journey now! John and Giselle are looking forward to greeting you in the places of your dreams.

Networking... The Natural Extension of You!

John and Giselle:

Everything great that we have ever done in life has been a team effort - the mini-network of John and Giselle. It has been a combination that has lead us to a life that we could never have imagined. This book is also a team effort so we will jump back and forth, each of us telling certain experiences and relating principles and strategies that moved our networking force forward. There were events that affected the two of us differently, and our evolution in the business was quite unique with each of us driving the ship at various times. Giselle is the visionary and energy plug for our team and John is the practical, step-by-step implementor. Our combined effort has been a winning network that we have been able to extend throughout the United States, Canada, the Orient and which will continue to expand throughout the world. No longer are we just a team of two, we have naturally extended ourselves to an almost limitless number. Our network has created for us wonderful associations, great friendships, and a life that is full and exciting. Sit back and enjoy the journey with us, but be ready to get out of your chair and start making things happen to "naturally" extend yourself to a higher level through networking.

Giselle:

Networking is based on the concept of synergy, which simply stated, is one plus one equal three or more! Now math has never been my favorite subject so this equation was quite exciting to me. I started to look at the numbers and how by adding just a few people to our network we could see incredible change. Look at it this way; if you take 3x3x3x3x3x3 you get 729 and then you add just one little number to it and try 4x4x4x4x4x4 you get 4,096! The difference of extending yourself by just one is 3,367! This is what networking is all about. This applies to everything in life from extra time to extra dollars to extra joy and fulfillment. The best way to enjoy your life is to extend yourself to others and the best way to do that is through networking.

John:

I was at the bank making a deposit of the check Giselle and I had just received from our network headquarters when I began to reflect on the amazing changes that had taken place in our lives over the past four years. I casually set the deposit slip on the counter and waited for the middle-aged teller to come to the window to serve me. He picked up the deposit slip and the check and did a double - and then a triple-take of the numbers on the slip and check. They did match up, they were correct, and they were big. His eyes grew rounder as he looked up at me and said, "Wow! This is more money than I will probably make in my entire life." I laughed and told him that he was only applying himself as one person. I also told him he could make the same money as Giselle and I, if he would look outside himself, leverage himself and work with others.

Back in the car and heading for home, I reflected on the words of the teller. I had once been doing the same kind of thing, working all alone to support myself and my family. I thought back to the long hours and never-ending struggle of running my retail stores and all of the headaches that went along with it. I thought about the deposit that I had just made. It was a months worth of effort that equated to more than I used to make in a year! I was a little amazed myself. How did it happen?

I had often heard that you can have anything you want, if you help enough other people get what they want. It made good sense to me, but for many years I only applied it in terms of working as an individual in a business. Then it hit me. NETWORKING... A Natural Extension of You! For years I was doing it the long and hard way, trying to do things one at a time and all by myself, just like the teller at the bank. Networking allows me to help more and more people get what they want because Giselle and I have an entire team to assist us in our mission. The more people we help get what they want, the more we get what we want.

The Natural Extension and Evolution of Our Network

John and Giselle:

We are excited to have the opportunity to share with you some of the dynamic lessons learned over the past seven years in networking. We are confident that if you can internalize and implement the strategies contained in this book that you can change your life for the better. As we begin our journey, we would like to give you a quick view of where we are, where we came from, and where we are going with this exciting business of networking.

John grew up in Canada and Giselle grew up in Puerto Rico. We didn't have any special training or education before we started in this business. John had a twelfth grade education and had been financially successful in an international manufacturing business. Giselle had worked in accounting and bookkeeping before returning home to be a full-time mother. We lived in Stuart, Florida and thought we were doing a pretty good job of pursuing our American dream.

Giselle:

I remember when John called and said he was flying home early from a trip in Canada so that we could take a look at a new business. I thought to myself, "Oh great, another deal." I picked John up at the airport and he proceeded to share all of his excitement about the network marketing organization. I listened to him patiently and as soon as he finished I went into the old, "over my dead body" routine. Fortunately, John was committed and filled out the distributor agreement, which I refused to sign, and he sent it off to headquarters.

We got some of the product and it seemed to be very high quality, but I just couldn't accept that it was a truly great product because it was not offered at Bloomingdales or Saks.

I began to use these products that were developed in Europe and they gave me some tremendous results. I was still totally against the business but gained a little bit of confidence when my hair dresser asked what on earth I had been using on my hair and where could she get it so that she could sell it in her salon. I quickly told her that she didn't want to offer it in her salon because she would have to sign all of these forms and become a distributor, etc., etc.

I came home and told John that I had found someone to be a distributor in his network. After listening to my story he said, "That's great! I am leaving town tomorrow and I want you to do what you did with your hair dresser today with as many other salons as you can in Stuart before I get back!"

My chin hit the floor and I said, "Forget it!"

John went on to say how easy it would be and that he knew I could do it. When I refused again he said, "Come on I am going to show you how easy it is right now."

We jumped in the car, drove into the city and pulled up in front of a barber shop. John walked in boldly and I stood cautiously at the door. As John began to explain about the wonderful product and what it could do for his customers the man just stared at John like he was some sort of alien. He then rather forcefully asked us to get out of his building.

We went back to the car and I sat down in a very pouty way and started to give John the "I told you so" line as best I could. He casually replied that I just couldn't take the rejection personally and that things would get better as we went along.

We pulled up to the next salon and John looked over and said, "O.K. now it is your turn."

I quickly fastened my seat belt and said, "There is no way I am going in there." John just sat there for a few moments and then said that I had a choice. I could go in there on my own or he would carry me in kicking and screaming. I chose the first option and slowly and reluctantly walked into the salon. The person behind the counter was very friendly and after I had stood there in silence for what seemed to be an eternity, she asked me if I needed an appointment. I broke down and quickly said, "No, no, my husband is out in the car and he won't let me go home until I tell you about this great product that will be wonderful for your customers." The person behind the counter hadn't understood a word I had said. She replied, "I'm sorry, is there something I can do to help you?" I tried to catch my breath and spoke a little bit slower, but not much. She said it sounded interesting and asked if I had any brochures. I said, "No, but I will find some and send them to you in the mail." With that I quickly ran out the door to the car. It was a long ride home.

John began by using evenings and weekends to work on the business and I watched with much skepticism, which of course I shared with him at every opportunity. I'll never forget the day we received our first check. I opened the envelope to find a whopping $50.00. I couldn't believe that John had spent so much time for such a little reward. I told him he was wasting his time, money and energy and that I wondered if he had lost all of his common sense.

The months went by and the checks remained quite low for the next four months. The fifth month I opened up the envelope expecting to see another small dollar reward for John's countless hours of work. I was truly amazed to see that we had made several thousand dollars. I quickly ran to John and asked him if this was legal. He assured me that this was the finest company with the finest products and that was why it worked. He was glad to see that I was excited about the business. At this point I was excited and became somewhat of a partner... I committed myself to spending the money that John made. It seemed like a great partnership.

John:

By 1987 Giselle was starting to take note of my personal growth and the size of our monthly checks. She began testing more and more of the products and loved the results.

Finally, she decided on her own that she would become a distributor as well. Giselle called the home office and added her name to what became "our" business. She did a little here and there as she was raising our small children, and before long, she became a driving force in our business. Giselle began to see how this wonderful product combined with the power of the network was making a tremendous difference in the lives of many individuals.

To this point I was working the business part time and still running my manufacturing company. In June of 1988 we were returning from the company convention when I decided that it was time to move into networking full-time. Our income dropped significantly. As our income dropped, we could not support the kind of lifestyle that we were accustomed to, nor could we support our credit cards, so we did the American thing and ordered a few more credit cards.

There were many late nights driving to Miami or other cities to help our network conduct meetings. Often we wouldn't get home until the wee hours of the morning, get up after only a few hours sleep and head off in another direction to conduct another meeting. Our friends were laughing at us and saying things like, "How could you be so foolish as to get into a business like that? This is never going to work." Our family even started to shake their heads in bewilderment of the path we were taking.

After two years in the business we were still struggling to make ends meet. We had a balloon payment coming up on our home and things were looking pretty bleak. I didn't have a penny coming in from any other source and I was getting extremely nervous.

We ran some ads in different areas and began to go through our contacts and see what we could find. Slowly we turned the corner and got some positive momentum going. Within 18 months our monthly checks were exceeding the amount that I used to make in an entire year.

John and Giselle:

We had learned to extend ourselves through the power and dynamics of the network. The rewards of this effort have been incredible. We have met some of the greatest people in the world and have adopted many of them not only into our network but more importantly into our circle of family. This is a family business. You start as a little family and can expand to unbelievable numbers.

Now we have a life without stress. We have the freedom to do as we wish. We are able to be with our children all of the time and be involved in their lives and interests and watch them grow and develop like never before. We enjoy a beautiful home in a great community, with no mortgage. We didn't realize that this was even an option a few years ago. Using our freedom like a library card we have traveled throughout the world enjoying all that it has to offer.

We started this business from our kitchen counter and that is where we run it today. No need for an office! No need to fight traffic to get to work! No bookkeeping! No accounting! Best of all, our children are involved in what we do and we are always there for them when they have a need!

Networking has helped us become better parents, better friends, better citizens and better individuals. It is often said that the best way to build a better world is to build a better you. Networking will assist you in building a better you and a better world. Networking is truly the best thing that ever happened to us and maybe after reading this book, it will become the best thing that ever happened to you. As you read about some of the specifics of our journey to success, commit to implement the principles in your own life whether you are in an organized networking company or not. We hope that they will change your life for the better in the same way they have changed our lives.

It is Harder to Fail than to Succeed!

John:

Everyone always talks about the high price of success, achievement and financial freedom. I think that they are painting an inaccurate picture. We have learned, and strongly believe, that it is harder, more frustrating and more expensive not to succeed than it is to succeed.

While on a cruise with the family I learned a lesson that has been a guiding force for me. Everything was going great with everyone having a marvelous time enjoying the warm sun and the fresh sea air, when it happened. The children had discovered that the cruise offered jet ski rentals for riding in the beautiful deep blue ocean around the ship. They wanted to go so badly. Again and again they pled and begged me to take them out so I quickly ran back to the cabin to ask Giselle how our credit cards were holding out. I already knew the answer but I put the question to Giselle anyway. She responded with her usual positive outlook, "We are close to being totally maxed out, but I am sure we can make it home, O.K." Upon my asking which card had the most room left, she reluctantly handed me the Visa and said, "Be careful, we really do need to make it home!" I walked back to the jet ski rental desk calculating how long I would be able to rent the jet ski for the kids. I have never been real big on math but even I was surprised when I discovered that I could only afford to take them out for twenty minutes!

I tried to make it sound positive but I could see the look of disappointment on the kids faces as I stepped to the counter and tried to confidently and unashamedly say, "I would like to rent a jet ski for 20 minutes." Even the clerk was embarrassed as she outfitted us with life jackets and led us to exactly twenty minutes of fun and adventure.

One kid at a time, I steered the jet ski around the boat, keeping my eye on the clock and trying to disregard the sinking feeling in my stomach as each begged to extend his turn just a little bit longer. The kids could sense my tense and upset posture as I tried to hurry them on and off the jet ski. As expected, the time went quickly and jet skiing was over. What was not over was the dissatisfaction of each of my children echoing in my mind the remainder of the trip and throughout the following several weeks. It was then that I decided and resolved that I would never again live with the anguish of not being able to do something I truly wanted to do for my family. It was just too great a price for me to pay. I was motivated to make my life my own and gain a full understanding of who I was and what I wanted to become. It was so much harder and more painful for me to experience failure than the pain of any work I have ever put into my business.

A poet wrote, "Of all sad words of tongue and pen, the saddest are these - It might have been."

It is a much more painful existence to live in wonder of what could have been than it is to go out and pay the price of success with blood, sweat, and tears. In our training seminars and opportunity meetings for potential associates we often ask participants if they would take a job shoveling manure for $20,000 or more a month. They usually think it through quickly, calculate what they would do with the $240,000 plus dollars a year and reply with a resounding "yes." We then explain to them that shoveling manure is a lot like running an effective business; You have to shovel a ton and get sweaty and smelly and even get a few blisters, but by doing so you will enjoy success and the financial rewards that follow.

We see so many individuals sitting on the side line watching and wishing that they could be a super-star player and enjoy the freedom that comes from success. It is hard to sit on the bench and view the excitement and thrill of an all-American lifestyle, especially when you recognize that you have the power and the potential. I challenge you to find the courage to discover the real you.

It is harder to fail than to succeed. It is like the lazy person who does "nothing" for a living; he can't take a break and get a rest because he isn't doing anything to begin with. All he can do is wonder about what might have been. This, too, is actually more tiring than a twelve or fourteen hour work day. People who do nothing feel boxed in and stagnate. This is where the life of quiet desperation begins. Not succeeding puts much more of a physical, emotional and psychological strain on our lives than any amount of work toward success. You truly must gain the desire to get out of the grand stand and on to the playing field of life.

As you strive to build your business, keep in mind the fact that it is more difficult to fail than to succeed. One of the most often used excuses we hear from potential distributors and individuals who are not paying the price of success is, "I just can't afford to spend the time, spend the money, take the chance or make the commitment, right now." The reality is that no one, you or any one else, can afford not to!! Many people use the same excuses of not enough time or money when talking about their health and fitness. They say that they are too busy to exercise and eat right. Again, the reality is that if they would take the time to exercise and eat right they would have more energy, be more productive and more effective in every aspect of their life. You really can't afford not strive for the best that is in you. In networking and life you must make the time to succeed and avoid putting things off for another day.

Don't buy into excuses, especially your own. Success doesn't come easy and requires that you take action even when you are afraid or discouraged. Resolve and commit right now, today, to get out there and make it happen and discover how much freedom and satisfaction you can enjoy by using the natural extension of you - Networking!

You Can't Cry While Riding a Bicycle

Giselle:

While growing up, I was very fortunate to have a grandmother who was committed to helping me become my best. Many are the lessons I learned from her, but none is greater than the lesson that came on a hot summer day in my native land of Puerto Rico.

I am not sure if the major factor was being a nine-year-old, the incredible heat, my stubbornness, boredom or all of the above. Probably all of the above, but I had had it with everyone in the house. I was fighting with the family, whining and pouting about anything that came up and generally just looking for an argument. Of course it didn't take long and I had found one and unfortunately, or perhaps fortunately, I lost the argument and began to cry and pout.

No one could get me to stop crying. They tried to bribe me with treats and promises to be nice and everything else they could think of but to no avail. I wouldn't stop and began to escalate my demonstration to even louder cries and more obnoxious screams. My grandmother watched patiently, as always, somehow hoping that someone would figure out the solution recognized by her from the beginning. After a long wait she finally arose from her chair, took me by the hand and walked me out to the garage.

I fought her most of the way complaining that I wanted to stay inside and I didn't want to go with her. We walked through the cluttered garage and came to my rusting red bicycle. Grandma stopped and said nothing. I wasn't sure what we were doing in the garage and why we were standing over my bicycle. I looked up into her large olive eyes and understood the silent command to get on the bike and ride.

I continued to sniff and tried to wipe away a few of the tears that were streaming down my face as I bent over, picked up my bike and started to ride down the dusty street. The further I rode, the more my tears subsided. I caught my breath and inhaled deeply as I picked up speed going down one of the many rolling hills in our neighborhood. The more I peddled, the better I felt. Before long I was whistling a tune and waving to my friends as I passed them on the street.

After a long and joyous ride, I pulled back up to the house to find grandma waiting for me on the front steps. I sat down beside her and she softly whispered, "Remember that you cannot cry while riding a bicycle." I didn't understand what she meant then, but today this principle is a driving force in my personal life and in our business.

To put grandma's philosophy into some very simple terms, "You can't be depressed when you are taking action." "You cannot gripe or complain when you are working on your loftiest goals." And, "You can't be sad when you are looking for the good and happy things in life."

If you truly desire to build a successful business, you must be committed to take action. Action is the key to any business, especially network marketing. You can't just sit and think about success or how you are going to make and spend your millions. You have to get off of your duff and make it happen. The more you sit around and don't take action, the less likely you will be to take action and you will soon be in a deep rut.

who struggle in this business are the ones who sit around and complain about their up-line, down-line or the company as a whole. They try to bring others into their circle so that they can validate their own poor performance or lack of success. They create the group griping and pity parties that literally knock countless individuals out of the business and prevent them from attaining their goals and dreams.

When successful distributors start to feel like procrastinating their calls or training meetings, putting off their follow-up calls, or feel like complaining about the people in their organization, they know that this is the time to double their efforts, try even harder and commit to taking even more action. They know that you can't feel down when you are taking action. Action will lead to desired results when complaining, crying and moaning won't.

The story is often told of the man who lived in a fine home and who was very successful and was faithful in praying morning and night. One rainy day the waters rose and began to spill from the rushing rivers. The water came into the man's home so of course the man began to pray that he would be saved. As the water filled the house an alert was sounded for everyone to leave the area. A patrol car came by the man's home and called for him to jump into the jeep to be taken to higher ground. The man shouted back that he was praying and that he was sure that the Lord would save him. The rushing waters continued to swell as the dam burst sending additional water towards the man's house. He climbed onto the roof and continued to pray. Soon a boat came by and offered him a quick ride to safety but again the man replied that he was praying fervently and was sure that he would be saved by a higher power. The water inched its way up the roof as the man climbed for the chimney. His prayers intensified and, as he poured out his heart, he was interrupted by the whirling of a helicopter just overhead. A rope was dropped, but he refused, convinced that his intense prayers would soon be heard. It wasn't too much longer when the water swept the man away drowning him in the flood. The man regained his senses as he met his Lord at the pearly gates. Angrily, the man shouted, "Why didn't you save me? I was faithful and I prayed with all the energy of my soul. Why didn't you answer my prayer?" The Lord calmly and gently replied, "I answered your prayer three times my son; I sent you a jeep, a boat and even a helicopter. Since you wouldn't take action, you paid the price that all who choose not to act must pay."

Not taking action will lead you down a path of misery, doubts and regrets. Many studies have been done on people who have lived to be 100. These centurions are often asked how they managed to live that long and what they regret about their lives. Almost without exception they attribute their longevity to staying active and taking action on a regular basis. They have goals and dreams that keep them busy and focused on the positive side of life. Those who aren't action oriented tend to get down and depressed about growing old and give up on themselves long before their bodies and minds are ready.

When asked about their regrets over their long lives, the responses always center around things they didn't do or try. Rarely, if ever, did a regret involve something they did, but things they knew they could have done had they only tried - things like getting more education, taking more time with family, trying new and interesting hobbies, etc. etc. It is true, the things we don't do usually keep us guessing and wondering about what we could have done.

In a recent training meeting for distributors, a lady came up to me after, complimented me on my presentation and said that she was literally amazed at my enthusiasm. Another lady just behind her leaned in and said, "Well, it is easy to be motivated when you are making the kind of money Giselle is making." The comment upset me a lot and caused me to reflect on the events of the past seven years.

As I drove home, I pondered the lady's comment and reflected on my attitude about life and work. Was I up-beat and enthusiastic because of my bank account? Was I dynamic because I had built a business that was giving me all the freedom and joy I had dreamed? Upon arriving home I rushed into the house and went to the storage room and began to dig through box after box of items we had collected over the life of our business. Finally, I found what I was looking for - a cassette tape recording of a training meeting I had given about five years ago! I knew that we weren't making any money to speak of through the business at that time so it would answer the question of the source of my energy.

I sat in front of the tape recorder and was a little hesitant about placing the cassette inside. I decided to go for it and quickly slammed it in and pressed the play button. It seemed like an eternity before I heard my voice come on, but to my relief and excitement, I sounded even more up-beat and enthusiastic in that meeting than I did today.

This solidified in my mind the need for action. I knew that the reason I had enthusiasm then and why I still have it today is because I am committed to take action and to take it now! Whining, worrying and whimpering will never lead you to success. In fact, they will lead you in exactly the opposite direction. Take action and the world will seem right, bright and ready to blossom.

Where are you today? Are you taking action and building the life you desire? Are you standing in the corner whimpering and crying or are you getting on your bicycle and making things happen?

Wherever you might be today in your business or personal life there is a bicycle waiting for you one that will take you anywhere you want to go. The only thing you have to do is get on and ride.

Commit today to take action by writing down the next ten action steps you are going to take in building your business or developing your personal life. They don't have to be big and overwhelming activities, but they must require that you get going and going now!

Stop complaining and start training and gaining and moving in the direction of a life of success and happiness. You will come to find, as I did, that you can't be down and depressed about your business if you are out there trying. *You truly can't cry while riding a bicycle.!*

"I Planned it This Way!"

John and Giselle:

Watching the Hawaiian surf roll in softly against the sandy shore, we relaxed in our lounge chairs with the ocean breeze and warm sunshine showering upon us. We were at a convention with our network organization's leaders, truly basking in the thrill, excitement and adventure that had entered our lives. In one of the lounge chairs sat Blake R., the president of our organization. We were somewhat awed and inspired to be with him.

John:

I had been relaxing and just listening to bits of the conversation, when I realized this was a good time to pose a question I had been dying to ask Blake. "Blake, did you ever dream that you would be in the position you are today - running a multi-million dollar network organization with the freedom to buy, do and see anything in the world that you wanted?"

I sat back and half expected to hear Blake say that it was a miracle, that he didn't deserve it, and that he couldn't believe what had happened in his life. I was somewhat jolted when he very casually replied, "John, I planned it this way."

We like to think that great things just happen in life, but if you want to really succeed, you have to plan for it. There are a few who do win the lottery or are born with an enormous silver spoon in their mouth, but for most of us that isn't a reality, nor is it the way we would want to live our lives. Making a plan is a common strategy that all truly successful people employ. If you truly want to network and extend yourself to financial and personal freedom, you must begin by making a plan.

Making specific plans is a common trait of all peak performers and high achievers in this business and every business. For me the planning stage was easy to understand because I am analytical by nature, but that didn't help me to actually do it. It wasn't until Giselle and I actually jumped in with both feet and made specific plans that we started to succeed in the business.

Before you establish plans you must have a very clear picture of your present reality. It is like looking at the directory in a shopping mall. There are all kinds of fancy color codes and detailed maps of the stores, but the most important part of the whole thing is the brightly colored dot that says, "You Are Here!" It doesn't matter how wonderful your map, if you don't know where you are right now. We call this defining your present reality. Look at your goals and your potential plans and ask yourself, "Where am I today in relationship to the accomplishment of this goal?" Once you have identified where you really are, then you are truly ready to begin making a plan that will lead you on a course to success.

What kind of plans do you need to make? I suggest specific, time-framed, and emotionally charged plans. It is true that when we deal in generalities we rarely succeed; and when we deal in specifics we rarely fail. Most people who never make it in this wonderful world of networking fail because they work as wandering generalities rather than becoming a powerful specific. There is a certain magic about specifics that moves us toward the accomplishment of any goal. Take a moment right now and look at your business and identify some specific areas that you would like to improve. It could be new contacts, follow-ups, product knowledge, training for your people or opportunity meetings. Write down one that you can begin working on immediately. What are the specifics that need to be done? How long will it take you to do each step? Are there people who will help and support you in this? Is there any knowledge or skills you need to develop to accomplish the plan? These are just a few of the questions you should ask yourself before embarking on any plan or goal.

Giselle:

I had always heard that you should attend seminars if you want to improve yourself and succeed in life. I had also heard that seminars were a great place to make contacts and do some prospecting. I wasn't very sure of myself in the business and had never done anything at the seminars I attended. One night I was preparing to go to a motivational seminar and John suggested I plan to make some contacts. I didn't think I could do it and was very nervous, but I made a plan to take and distribute seven sample packets with my business cards. I knew what the plan was and committed myself to make it happen no matter what. It did make me a little less nervous about talking to people, but not much. I hesitated several times and probably missed a few good people; however, I stayed to the end of the meeting and finally handed out my seventh packet and ran for the door. I had done it and I was getting out of there!

A few days later John asked me how my follow-up plan for working the contacts from the seminar was going. What follow-up plan? I had accomplished my objective of placing the seven sample packets; what more did he want out of me? John gently informed me that the overall plan was to help people learn about the business and make a decision if it was the right career move for them. He helped me create a second plan to do follow-up calls to the seven contacts. Once that plan was set I was really scared because I didn't think I could do it. I am the person who wouldn't even sell girl scout cookies as a child because it was too uncomfortable for me. In fact, when the cookie sale would come around each year, I would get a sick feeling in my stomach and go home and cry to my parents that I just couldn't do it. They usually got all of my family and extended family to buy enough so I wouldn't have to go out and sell. Anyway, I looked at my plan for follow-up calls over and over again. I even dialed a few of the numbers and let it ring a time or two and then quickly hung up. I just couldn't do it. The plan lay there in front of me and wouldn't go away. I had made a commitment and knew that I couldn't rest with a clear conscience until I had completed my plan. The first few calls were extremely short. I would say in a very shaky voice, "Hi, this is Giselle Sexsmith, I met you at the seminar and gave you a sample of our product and I know you are very busy and I am sure you are not interested anyway, but I appreciated your time and call me if you have any questions, Good-bye!" My heart would be racing a hundred miles an hour and it would take me a few minutes to catch my breath. Then I really had to psyche myself up for the next call. Finally, I got a little more confident as I worked my plan and my calls became a little bit more relaxed and lasted more than 20 seconds. By the time I got to the last couple of calls I was almost having fun. Sticking to my plan enabled me to actually sign up one new distributor. What a feeling that was. I know that planning for success isn't convenient and often is uncomfortable, but if you want to walk the beaches of the world you have to plan for it!

John:

Setting time frames and creating an emotional charge are the critical factors to planning and succeeding in this business. I think one of our greatest experiences was in planning to have as many of our executives become "Blue Diamonds," the highest achievement level in the company, the year after we had done it. Our plan was to have 12 of them make it and that was a very lofty goal. We started to break things down and really look at what it would take to make this plan a reality. What were the key issues? What did we have to do to support, encourage and empower our people to do what we had done? We started with the time frame of one year. It seemed long enough and we felt we could create an action plan that would carry us there. Then we knew we needed to create an energy and urgency that would get all of us to take action. We took the picture that was taken at the convention when we became Blue Diamonds and sent it with a simple message, "Now it is your turn!" We sent these to the down line executives and our plan was that 12 of them would become Blue Diamonds by the next convention. Then we started to work our plan. Almost a year to the day we sat and watched as a total of 17 individuals became Blue Diamonds and walked proudly across the stage!

The old saying is true that you must plan your work and work your plan. If you are ready to walk the beaches of the world and enjoy the sunshine on the mountain tops of success, achievement and happiness, plan it that way and work it that way. Where will you be three months, six months and one year from today? Plan for it and begin making it happen today!

You Can't Start Out In Fourth Gear

Giselle:

I think it is unfortunate that so many people who come into the business of networking want to start out making incredible amounts of money and living a dreamy life style. It is important to recognize that it takes time, energy and a lot of hard work to get to a level of success. You simply do not land on top of a mountain and you do not start at a speed of 65 miles an hour. You must build your way to success. Our business is often called a vehicle to success.

Now, I am no mechanic, but I have learned a few things about vehicles that relate directly to succeeding in this business.

I learned this lesson in Puerto Rico when I was sixteen years old. I wanted to learn to drive but the only car we had was an old stick shift. I had seen some of my friends and my older sister drive and I had a vivid image that I could do it. However, no one else thought I could do it, and I must admit that for a while I believed them and didn't think I could do it myself. Then I began visualizing myself succeeding and pictured myself in the car driving all over town and having a great time. I started to believe that I could do it, and then I knew I could do it.

I had a hard time convincing my family that I could drive the stick shift on the hilly roads of our city but finally got them to give me a chance. My father finally agreed to be the guinea pig and took me out for my first drive. We hadn't gone very far when the car started to jerk and sputter and stall. There were cars honking and people shaking their fists at us. I broke down and couldn't do it. There was a lot of pain in that experience but the image of driving around the city was still greater in my mind than the pain of failure. My father took me to a nice, flat parking lot and we began our lessons. Before long I felt I was ready to get back out on the road. I started out a bit nervous about making a mistake but proceeded in a fairly smooth fashion. My visualization was paying off. I thought I had it down to a science when we came to a stop sign on a hill. I tried to relax and think about making the quick shift from brake to gas pedal and releasing the clutch all in time so that I wouldn't roll down the hill. I started to go and the car died. I knew I had done it correctly- how could the car have stopped? I quickly started the car and tried again. Same result, the engine killed. A third time, and again the same result. I was really frustrated now and was beginning to panic. My father then grabbed the stick shift and casually said, "You can't start out in fourth gear." I had been trying to start in a gear that was good only when you are up and running at a good speed.

We often do the same thing in our lives as we try to enjoy the rewards of success before we pay the price and get up to the speed of success. John and I went through first and second gear in our business several times before we actually got up to speed and moving in third and fourth gear. A couple of times we tried to shift our lifestyle before we shifted our work and business style so we always ended up stalling out and going back down to a lower gear.

Then we made the big jump! We were ready and were committed to take all the necessary steps in order to get to the higher gears in our vehicle for success. We quickly found out that there is definitely a price to be paid for success. It is a payment that is never paid in full because you have to make it every single day.

I remember early on how I drove to Fort Lauderdale every week to attend opportunity meetings. It took a lot of time to drive there every week which caused me to leave early and often return home very late at night. I remember a particular time when our daughter, Ninna, was sick. I had committed to take several people with me to the opportunity meeting and I didn't want to go. I was worried about my Ninna; I wanted to stay and be there with her. Another side of me knew I had made a commitment and that I needed to follow through if I was ever going to move our business to the next gear and level. We had Ninna checked, and I knew she was going to be all right. I also knew that she was in very capable hands with our helper and that John would be returning home shortly after I left. Still, I didn't want to go. I wanted to stay home. Then it was almost a voice that said, "Ninna will be fine. You made a promise to yourself and to others. Now stick to it, pay the price, and enjoy the rewards that follow." I hesitantly left the house and began picking people up. We made the long drive to Fort Lauderdale and the entire way all I could think about was my little girl who was sick. As soon as we got to the hotel where the meeting was being held, I dashed to the phone and called to check on my baby. Everything was fine. The meeting started and was about fifteen minutes old when I jumped out of my seat and ran back to the phone. Again Ninna was fine. I continued to do this every fifteen or twenty minutes for the entire meeting. When I got home, I was exhausted mentally and physically. Ninna had slept almost the entire time I was gone. Her fever was down and she was on the road to recovery. Plopping into bed, I had a wonderful feeling of accomplishment as I reflected on my willingness to pay the price. I realized that when you put things in order and live up to your commitments and promises you can make incredible things happen.

What are the things that you need to do to take your business to a higher level? Take a few moments right now and make a list: "Things that I am not doing right now" that I need to be doing to move to the next level. I'll give you a hint; *It is usually the little things that either hold us back or propel us forward to the accomplishment of our goals and dreams. In this business, the little things are crucial.*

If you are straining in first gear right now, take a challenge for the next two weeks to evaluate where you are and create some specific action plans for each of the fourteen days. This usually creates a shift as you pay the price for success. The results are not always immediate, but trust me when I say that there are no short cuts to success in this business. There is an order that you need to follow to get from first gear to second, then to third, fourth and finally into overdrive.

Every industry goes through a similar process of stages and gear shifts before they become really effective and successful. The four stages or gears are: innovation, infrastructure, regulation and diversification. There are some wonderful examples of all four stages in the automotive industry. First there was the innovation stage where the product was created, the first automobile was built. People usually think that things are just a fad or passing fancy and that they won't survive. It is like the blacksmith who laughs as he sees the car rumbling down the rocky road and continues to pound out horseshoes. (Often the people who are innovation bashers end up on the outside looking in and wondering what might have been!) Shifting to the infrastructure stage we see the development of many facilities or services that support the innovation. For the automobile this included the building of better roads, gas stations, the assembly line for production, better equipment and so on. Then the regulators and law makers step in to "protect the public." For the automobile they came in and established some very interesting laws and ordinances. One state law required that anyone who was driving a car to have a responsible adult running out in front of it waving a red flag, shouting a warning that the car was coming. Another law required that if a car encountered a horse, the owner of the car was to immediately stop the car and hide it behind the nearest tree or bush so as to not scare the horse. These kinds of laws are usually short lived and usually are cause for a good laugh over the long haul. The fourth gear of diversification is the expansion of the product lines and the opportunity for incredible growth.

Networking has gone through this same kind of evolution and gear shifting. Networking started out with a majority of people in business and industry discounting it as only a passing fancy and expected it to run its course and die a natural death in a very short period of time. Many of those so called experts are on the outside looking in and wishing they had gotten involved. Then the infrastructure was created with automatic accounting, shipping and processing. This freed the distributors to spend their time doing what they do best rather than worrying about a lot of little details. Right now there are a lot of interesting laws and regulations being created, some of which are a little humorous and some that will strengthen the industry as a whole. A few companies, like ours, have made the shift to full scale diversification of products and opportunities. This shift has created some of the most enormous opportunities for success, wealth, and service ever. We are riding high in this gear and the turbo charge and overdrive are creating energy, action and change that is revolutionizing direct sales as we know it.

Another way to look at it is this: When you start the business in first gear, you travel slowly and often don't get paid for your efforts and the time you put in. Then as you move along into second and third gear you start getting paid for your efforts and all the work and time you give to building your business. Then when you get into fourth gear and overdrive you have momentum to keep things rolling and moving in a positive direction. This business is much like a space craft taking off where almost 90% of the effort and fuel consumption comes in the first few seconds of lift off. Much energy is expended as you try to break the gravitational pull of the earth. Then, once you get beyond lift off, it takes very little effort and energy to keep positive things happening. This is a business of momentum and focus and you make it happen one step at a time.

It all comes down to paying the price and being willing to move from one step to another in sequence. When you are down or a little discouraged, turn on an after burner and make a more concerted effort to succeed.

Budgeting
For
Success

John:

When Giselle and I married, she begged me for a long time to sit down and set up a budget. The idea wasn't very appealing to me and I resisted it. Finally I consented and we sat down to begin the process. Giselle began our discussion by asking what the budget limit was and how much money did we have to spend. I thought about it for a minute and the thought of being limited to that budget did not sit well with me at all. I turned to her and said, "You tell me how much you want to spend and I will create the means to make it happen." I could have knocked her over with a feather. It hadn't occurred to her, at that point in time it hadn't occurred to me, that you could set up a budget based on what you wanted rather than based on what you had.

Take a look at your life right now. How does it look to you? What kinds of things would you like to have and do today? What kinds of things would you like to have and do over the next three months? Stop reading and take fifteen minutes and create a budget for yourself based on what you want and not on what you have. Don't worry if they don't match right now because they probably won't if you are like most people. Remember, I am not suggesting that you spend what you don't have. I want you to begin to create the abundance that will allow you to get what you want. Now take a few moments and evaluate your performance and identify what you need to change to bring your performance into harmony with your desire. How many more people do you need to recruit, how much more training do you need to do with your new people, what follow-up do you need to do with your executives, and what encouragement do you need to give to everyone? How much product do you need to move either through your retail customers or your direct distributors? Remember that the only way to really make it in this business is to move quality products to end users. The product makes the difference. Now get out of your chair and go do it. It is the only way to live your life based on a desire based budget.

Another facet of budgeting is evaluating how you spend your energy, both physical and mental. As you look at what you want, you have to budget for the amount of energy and time it is going to take you to achieve your desired result. We spend far too much time and energy on things that don't lead us to success and achievement. Most of us operate on the 80-20 principle, which means that 20% of what we do in activity generates 80% of our results. Unfortunately this also means that we spend 80% of our time doing very little in terms of production. There are many things that can really drain your budgeted energy supply. One "Drain" is what you worry about. We spend far too much time worrying about things that we can't control. Studies have shown that almost 96% of the things we worry about never actually happen. What a waste of energy, focus and time! Commit to budget your energy on the things you can control and the things that will lead you to success. Another possible "Drain" on our energy supply is the people we associate with. Negative people can really drain your energy and distract you from you goals and dreams. We will talk more about this in a later chapter. As you budget for success make sure that you are protective of your energy supply and your time. Budget for success by investing in quality, productive time and using your energy to launch yourself into the winners circle of achievement.

You will feel more freedom and less stress as you increase your ability to do what you want. No longer will you have to think about the "what ifs" and "if onlys" that follow most people throughout their lives. You can take control. Take control today! You can make it happen and live a life that is truly worth living and experience all the good things that life has to offer.

A Tight Rope
To Success

John:

I have always been fascinated with the circus. I love all the variety, the flair and excitement of the Big Top. In particular, I love to watch the tight rope walkers. They truly have nerves of steel and are able to focus all of their energies toward the accomplishment of their goal. It always amazed me that they would never look down at the wire. They never once looked down to see where they were going to place their next precious step. Always they focused solely on the platform on the other side of the wire. They would move along slowly and cautiously with their eyes fixed on the goal, never wavering from their plan and purpose.

Let me share the reason why tight rope walkers don't look down. "Down" is where the consequences of failure lurk. Down is not where they want to go. Across is the direction to which they are committed. In fact, I once heard a tight rope walker say that when a tight rope walker looks down he is certain to fall. Many studies have shown that you cannot concentrate on the opposite of an idea. If you are told to try as hard as you can not to think of an elephant, you are almost certain to do just that. In order to succeed you have to be focused on your success and not what might happen if you fail.

I see this in our business all of the time. People are so afraid to make a mistake or fail. We really have been over programmed in our society that it is bad and awful to fail at anything. The truth is that if you want to succeed you must be willing to fail. Failure is vital to success! All of the great accomplishments in history have come only after much failure. Babe Ruth, Thomas Edison, Abraham Lincoln and many others have failed countless times before they reached their goals and dreams. The reason they were able to persevere was their ability to focus on their goals and not on what would happen if they failed.

You will experience set backs and failures in this business. It is part of playing the game. Remember that they are only temporary detours on your journey to success. The important thing is that you take responsibility for your actions, learn from them and move onward and upward to success and achievement. Don't try to blame others. When you experience obstacles take time to reflect on the actions that led to the undesirable result. Then, map out a new course with strategies that will take you in the direction you want to go.

Many people simply do not want to take any risk and just want to stay where they are. These are the people who work to maintain the "status quo." Unfortunately, life is like riding a bicycle up a hill: You cannot stay in one place. If you are not moving up you are going down. Abraham Lincoln understood this principle. During the early years of the civil war Lincoln went through general after general trying to find one that could carry out his aggressive plan. The generals during those early years had an attitude of "protect the North." Lincoln's vision was to unify the nation. Not until Lincoln teamed up with General Grant was the mission accomplished. Don't be content to spend your time, effort and energy defending the status quo and get across the tight rope to your dreams.

All too often we focus on the consequences of failure instead of looking at what will happen when we succeed. Skeptics are wonderful at this kind of focus because it validates their speculation and justifies their poor performance. They come in with an attitude of "This business will never work," or "Well, I will try it for a month and see what happens." They are focused on the negative and that is exactly what they create - negative, failing results. Then when they don't succeed in the business they can easily say, "I just knew it wouldn't work for me." These "complainers" blame their poor performance on the company or the program. These individuals are much like our youngest son Jian James when he was being potty trained. We had gone through all the usual rituals of trying to get him out of diapers and into "big boy pants." We were working hard but weren't having much success, and Jian James was having no success at all. One day we sat him on his little potty chair and encouraged him to show us what a big boy he was. Jian James gave it his all. He grunted and groaned and winced his face as only a small child can. Then he stood up, looked at the empty container and said, "This potty doesn't work!" In this business you are responsible for making things happen. The system does work, and you must go beyond complaining about how it won't work and start working to make it work. Success in this business is up to you! The reality is that if individuals would focus on the positive and their goals for improvement, they would move in that direction and begin to see positive results. Be bold, take action and get on the line. It is the only way to achieve. Remember, negatives are never positives in networking or any other business.

Giselle:

Another key to focusing on the positive goal is to not reward the negative. Far too often we reward the whiner and crier with sympathy or additional justification for their lack of success. All this does is reinforce their negative behavior because you have validated their performance.

When someone calls me with complaints about their down-line or up-line or the people in their area, I try to turn their attention to what is going right for them or what is going right for someone else in their organization. In fact, I will begin every phone conversation with a positive story about someone in the network who has experienced some kind of success. This is a wonderful way to begin a conversation because it creates a positive focus on what great things we can do if we only apply ourselves. If the individual continues to pursue the negative I will listen and be attentive to their concerns. As a leader you must not just "blow off" the complaints or concerns of the people in the network. Once the individual feels that you have truly listened and understand their frustration then you can move them into a positive mode. The best way to do this is by focusing on the individuals personal strengths. Get them to take stock of their assets, things like their personality, their background or the contacts they have established. You can then get them to take positive action and focus on the responsibility they have for their own success. This is a business that requires you to take responsibility for your own actions. You can't blame anyone for your failure. It starts within. You will find a few people who are natural complainers. With these individuals the key again is to get them to focus on how many great things they have going for them and what a tremendous opportunity they have to reach their goals and dreams. You also need to point out that others who are in the same situation are succeeding! On occasion you may hit someone who just won't get of the complaining mode. I will often ask them to write everything down and send it to me. Usually once they start to write things down they realize that they are focusing on a silly and insignificant negative that is going to prevent them from achieving their goals. If you can get people to focus on why they can succeed, rather than why they cannot, you are sure to build a winning network.

It is also important to remember that you have to focus on the positive with people regardless of their performance. I have always said that it is impossible to scold someone to success. It cannot be done. It is like the old story of the

Wind and the Sun battling to see who was greatest. They argued back and forth until they finally decided to settle their argument with a contest. They saw a traveler walking down a winding road. They determined that who ever could get the clothes off of the traveler was the strongest and mightiest. The Wind went first and blew with all his might to get the clothes off the traveler's back. But, the harder he blew, the tighter the traveler clenched his coat about him. After some time he gave up exhausted. Then the Sun came out and gently shone upon the traveler and warmed him with its' rays. The traveler began to loosen his coat, and then his tie and before long he had stopped near a stream, taken off his clothes and cooled himself in the babbling water.

Trying to scold someone to success is operating in the same fashion as the Wind. The more you scold or criticize, the more people will guard themselves against you, resent you and refuse to work as a part of your team. On the other hand if you help them to focus on the positive and feel the natural warmth that comes with a job well done, they will listen to you, implement your advice and become a winning player on the team. It is all in your approach.

Are the people in your network focusing on the fear of failure or the benefits of success? It is vital that you create a climate for success. The only way to create the positive climate is by example. Help others be successful by being successful yourself. If you focus on the fear of failure that is what will be duplicated and passed down through the network. If you focus on the positive, it too will be passed on to every member of the team. You can do this by focusing on the little successes of the distributors. Help each person find a focus point of success and get them to commit to it. Write down the names of a few people who have had some little success and identify what you can do to validate their performance. Use the little successes to help them get their eyes focused in the direction of success and the life they truly want to live. Remember that you cannot give too much sincere praise. On his death bed the Duke of Wellington was asked if he would do anything different in his successful life. Everyone expected him to say that he would have done something to prevent the deaths of those who served under his command. Instead he replied, "I would definitely give more praise!" Praise helps people stay on the line and gives them the courage to continue to walk the tight rope of success.

The tight rope is where you are tested. It is only when you commit to walk that you discover your true strengths, weaknesses and abilities. By taking the risk to walk the tight rope you can find out who you really are and what you can do to truly become the best possible **you**! You are walking a tight rope each and every day and if you focus on the goal, you will win the prize.

Goose Sense

John:

Have you ever watched geese fly south for the winter? I am sure you have seen them flying in the "V formation." I have often wondered exactly why they fly that way and have found that their wisdom is worth emulating in the network marketing business.

Research has proven that geese fly in the V formation because they are able to fly at least 71% further in the formation than they could if they each flew individually. You see, as each bird flaps its wings it creates an uplift for the bird directly behind it. Whenever a goose falls out of formation, it immediately feels the drag of trying to go it alone and quickly falls back into formation. When the lead goose gets tired it rotates to the back and the next goose flies in the point position. It is also interesting to note the geese in the back honk continually as encouragement for those that are flying in the front. Geese have another fascinating practice. When a goose is sick or wounded, two other geese will fall out of the V and follow the ailing goose to the ground. They actually stay with that goose until it is able to fly again or dies. The two geese then form their own tandem to work their way back to their group or connect with another flock working its way south.

Interesting "Goose" information, but how does it relate to networking? In the following pages you will come to understand that if you have as much sense as a goose, you can survive and thrive in the dynamic world of networking.

The first facet of Goose Sense is synergy. Remember that synergy simply means that one plus one equals three or more. Geese can travel 71% further as a group than they can by themselves. This is the basis of networking. When you have a group of like minded, goal oriented individuals, you can get where you want to go at least twice as fast and most likely faster. You can also get where you want to go with less stress and pain because you can rely on the thrust of those around you to help keep you going. As you look to begin or improve your network, make sure that you look for positive people who will be team players and fly in formation for the benefit of everyone. This is a vital ingredient to being successful in this business.

The geese rotate the point position, which is the position that requires the most effort and energy. In your organization take turns doing the hard or tedious jobs that need to be done. This will not only assist everyone in keeping their energy and excitement up but will also be a vital element in creating new and stronger leaders for your network. When people know that they are an important part of a team, they tend to increase their performance level. People want to be associated with winners and will usually give you all they have in order to strengthen their standing in the team. Sharing the responsibility for some of your meetings and training seminars will create a thrust of energy into your network.

This next suggestion is vital to accomplishing your goals over the long journey. You must honk encouragement to all of your people, whether they are in the front or in the back. When you honk at your people, what message are you sending? Remember, you cannot scold someone to success nor can you develop a winning network with negative input. Be positive and up-beat with your people and make sure that you always build and encourage them to be their best. We will discuss this in more detail later.

Finally, we must have the same commitment to each individual as geese do. Just as a fallen goose is accompanied by two others, you too, must be willing to assist and aide those in your network who are struggling or have been wounded by a bad attitude or the dream stealers. Always be there for your people, especially when they are down. Nurse them back to networking health with some double doses of positive insight and information. Help them to work their way back to the rest of the group and get their network moving in a positive direction. This applies not only to those in your down-line, but to your up-line people as well. This is a team game and you cannot succeed without good people around you.

Giselle:

Another critical element for your network to fly in a powerful formation is to create a strong and common bond among your people. A formation of geese have a bond that holds them together through the winds and rains and the countless miles they travel to reach their destination. A bond among your network will help all of you to weather the storms of disappointment, rejection and life challenges and guide all of you to a wonderful and meaningful destination.

I really came to understand this principle of bonding while working with the Better Baby Institute in Philadelphia, Pennsylvania. They have done countless studies on the effects of bonding and the tragic consequences of not having bonding in children. They often refer to a historical account of Frederick II of Germany in which he conducted an experiment with orphaned babies. Frederick II wondered what language a baby would speak if no language was taught them in their early years. He wondered if they would speak Old Hebrew or some other dialect or if they would speak what their parents had spoken. He gathered up a group of orphaned infants and hired nurses to take care of and feed them. The nurses were not to speak or handle the infants, only to take care of feeding and changing needs. As the children developed they did not speak old Hebrew or any other language. They were very weak and withdrawn. They did not have a very strong life force and all died very young. It is true that without a bond and some personal attention, it is difficult to sustain meaningful life.

The people in your network need the same kind of attention and personal interest that an infant does. When distributors know that someone has a personal interest in them, they will perform and live in bolder and more productive ways. It is vital, too, that your interest is sincere. There is nothing worse than hollow or shallow praise. In most cases it is very offensive .

It is worth repeating over and over that if you are focused on the money aspect only, you will not last very long in networking. This is a people business and your whole focus must be to add value to the lives of others. It is so true, the only way to live a productive and happy life is by helping others help themselves. The money is a natural by-product of lifting others with the thrust of your wings and your vision.

In the ancient days of Rome the sculptors would often display a sign outside their shops which said, "Sina Cera." Translated this means without wax. It was a custom of some of the sculptors of the time to use wax instead of fine material. The wax would be dyed and usually looked finer than any other material. But of course, the wax statues and figurines would melt if you left them in the sun or in a hot room. Their beauty was short lived and their value diminished with the passing day. Only those statues that were carved out of fine materials like wood and stone would survive the heat of the day. The word Sina Cera is the basis for the English word sincere. With all of your people make sure that you base your bond on sincere praise and interest. Live your life and build your network without wax.

John:

Early on in our networking experience we were invited to the cabin of Craig B. When we arrived, I looked at the enormous wooden structure and changed the title from cabin to lodge. It was gorgeous and the surroundings were truly beautiful. We hadn't been there for very long when Craig pulled me aside and told me that he wanted me to view this "cabin" as my own and, further, any time I wanted to use it, just give him a call. To me he was demonstrating what the geese do for one another. He was sharing with me the fruits of networking before I had even developed them for myself. He was treating me like a brother or family member and that left a lasting impression on me and truly changed my impression of network marketing. This created a bond of friendship and sharing that has become a driving force for our network.

As you build your business, be sure to use some good old-fashioned "Goose Sense" and lift, build, support, sustain, encourage and bond with your people. If you use "Goose Sense," I am confident that you will fly high and strong into the upper echelons of networking success and achievement.

Overcoming
The
Dream Stealers

Giselle:

I am uniquely qualified to talk on the subject of dream stealing. During John's and my early days in the business, that was my role. We told this story at the beginning but I think it bears repeating to illustrate how dream stealers work and how to overcome them.

When John called and said he was flying home early from a trip in Canada to take a look at a new business. I remember thinking to myself, "Oh, great, another deal." I picked John up at the airport and he proceeded to share all of his excitement about the network marketing organization. I listened to him patiently and as soon as he finished I went into the old, "over my dead body" routine. Fortunately John was committed. He filled out the marketing agreement, which I refused to sign, and sent it off to headquarters.

John began by using evenings and weekends to work on the business. I watched with much skepticism which, of course, I shared with him at every opportunity. I'll never forget the day we received our first check. I opened the envelope to find a whopping $50.00. I couldn't believe that John had spent so much time for such a little reward. I told him he was wasting his time and energy. Dream stealers are great at pointing out the obvious and rubbing salt into open wounds. I was extremely good at it.

The months went by and the checks remained quite small until one day I opened up the envelope and found that we had made thousands of dollars in a single month. I quickly ran to John and asked him if this was legal, another typical dream stealer response. He assured me that this was the finest company with the finest product and that was why it worked. He then said something that is a wonderful thing to do with dream stealers. He stated how glad he was to see that I was excited about the business. At that point I was excited and became somewhat of a partner. You see, I committed to spend the money that John made. It seemed like a great arrangement. I continued to use the products, saw great results with them, witnessed John's success with our people and my dream stealing era came to an abrupt end.

It was kind of funny because no sooner had I stopped stealing John's dream that others tried to steal mine. Friends and neighbors literally laughed at our efforts to build our network. They thought we were crazy to chase from one city to the next doing meetings, getting up early and coming home late, all for the possibility of finding someone new to bring into the network. It was then that I really started to get it from my father. Every month he would call on the 20th, which happened to be the day we got our check. I know he wasn't doing it on purpose, but it was almost as though he was calling to confirm that we were failing in the business. He would always say that it was time for John and me to give up our foolishness and get back to a real job with security. Then came the month that we received our biggest check ever. I hurried and called my father in Puerto Rico to tell him the great news. He couldn't believe the amount of money we had earned. He then said, "Giselle, I have some advice for you so listen to me. It is time that you and John pick up and move to Utah and get the president of the network organization to give you and John jobs with a salary." I laughed and said, "Dad, you don't get it. Now that we have things going, they can't afford the kind of salary that would match what we can make here!"

John:

I had a similar dream stealing experience with a friend of mine. He too was skeptical about our involvement in networking and tried on several occasions to talk me out of it. He tried the same approach as Giselle's father and began calling me on the 20th of each month. He was getting the best of me for a while until our networking gained momentum and we started to see some results. Then the shoe was on the other foot and I began to call him on the 20th of each month to let him know what he had missed out on. He started calling the 20th of the month his "Hell Day." It is true that those who are the dream stealers are usually those who say, "I knew they would make it in the end."

The most important thing you can do in dealing with dream stealers is to make sure that your attitude is fixed on the positive and that you are firm in your resolve to make your network succeed. Of course the best approach of all is to avoid the dream stealers all together, but I realize that often in the early stages they may be someone you love, and I don't suggest you avoid them. Show your resolve and commitment to not let anyone pull you off track.

You must carefully choose those individuals with whom you are going to associate. If you wanted to go to medical school to become a successful doctor who would you associate with? Certainly you would not seek out individuals who had recently dropped out of medical school. You would find positive people who were either in, or who had successfully completed medical school. If you want to be a winner you must associate with winning people. Create a support system for yourself with positive, success oriented individuals who will help you avoid and overcome the dream stealers.

I have found that people who are focused on the money are the people who fall prey to the dream stealers most often. If money is your focus, you will never make it in this business. This business is about people and about product. Both the people and the product lead to better life styles for everyone involved. Together they are a dynamic duo that lead you to a better life.

You will without a doubt encounter a few, if not many, dream stealers along your journey to success. Pay them no heed. In fact encountering the dream stealers is an important mile marker. When this happens you know you are on the path to success. Keep focused on your goals and dreams and let them watch as you achieve a level of freedom and success that will leave them wishing and wondering.

Raising a Business

Giselle:

In the early days of our business, I was often scared and overwhelmed by what I needed to do to make the network grow and develop. I really doubted my ability to make a presentation, enroll new distributors, and motivate others to succeed. I didn't feel qualified. I certainly didn't have the skills or the training that would make me a superstar in this business.

Jerry C. and another up-line executive offered to take me to a training they were doing in a nearby city. I was amazed that two "high powered" individuals would be interested in helping me. They acted like my big brothers. I was nervous as I walked into the room and saw 35 unfamiliar faces staring at me. I sat down and began to question myself as to who I was kidding and what on earth I was doing at this meeting. Well, the program began and Clara M. stood up and addressed the group. I remember wishing that I had her talent and ability and longed to be able to experience her success. Clara's enthusiastic voice brought me back to reality as I caught her final sentence, "Building a successful network is just like raising a family!" That was it! I had five children and knew how to raise a family. I could succeed in this business. From that point on it was only a matter of putting the pieces together because I knew I had the formula for building a successful business - treat everyone like family.

I was so relieved to find out that you didn't ever have to use a "hard sell" or put the thumb screws on anyone. I was excited to know that I could build others up, support them, help them overcome challenges and learn how to succeed themselves. The longer we have been in this business the more firmly we believe that you must literally treat everyone in your network like family; and the truth is that they are. It is thrilling to see others grow and progress. I think that we get more enjoyment out of seeing our down-line people succeed than we do when we accomplish a new goal.

John:

This concept of raising a business is directly related to creating a culture within an organization. I have seen businesses around the world that have varied and diverse corporate cultures. The culture within your network is crucial to your long-term success. Culture is where the law of the harvest really comes into play. (You reap exactly what you sow).

Too many individuals get into networking because they feel it will be fast and easy money. As a result of this attitude they use a lot of promotion and hype in their meetings and paint the picture of get rich quick. They get their network to do a lot of "promotional" buying and their volumes soar quite rapidly. They experience great short-term growth and can make a lot of money. Then they fade quickly or completely disappear.

The saddest thing about this kind of culture is that it is passed on down the line to everyone who comes into the business. Down-line distributors are trained in the same way the original up-line person approached the business, and it is multiplied throughout that particular line of the network. The great power of the network is the ability to move information and methods through the system very rapidly. Thus, it is vital that only activities and information that strengthens the network should be passed along. The "bad" can travel down the network just as fast as the "good," and the effect it has on the overall culture can be devastating.

Within the network culture several factors must be present for the network to thrive over many years. Some of the most critical elements in creating the proper culture are: values, work ethic, support, and nurturing. Each play a vital role and all must be present in order to succeed.

Internal values are the core for success in this business. Far too many networking companies have lost their values as they have gone from one product to the next, from one scheme to another. They no longer care about individuals or quality products. This was one of the most important things we looked for before actually becoming involved in networking. Ethical practices begin with the parent company and with you. You have to be committed to run things in the proper way and resist the temptation of pushing people with heavy promotions and hype. It won't last and you may never be able to reclaim your network or your integrity from the effects of low ethics. It is a culture that is difficult to change once it has begun.

Having a solid work ethic creates a very professional culture within the network. If the people you sponsor into the business see you working hard and paying the price for success, they will likely follow your example. If they feel that you are just out to sponsor people and benefit financially and are never around when they need you, they will become cynical and develop work habits similar to yours. Your network is then on the verge of collapse.

Supporting people and determining where you spend your time are two crucial cogs in your network machine. Now, when I say support, I mean support of everyone in your business. It is easy to support those who are working hard and creating good results. In fact, working with people who are growing and improving is very intoxicating. You must, however, be in a constant mode of evaluating to make sure that you are spending your time on high production activities. Your activities must expand the network as a whole and lead the group to higher levels of success.

Your support of others is in constant transition and it requires that you ask yourself two critical questions; "Where do I spend my time?" and "Who is ready for my support?" The best way to evaluate where and with whom to spend your time is by looking at the distributors commitment. Support must be a parallel commitment. The distributor must invest as much into the business as you do. If you are expending more energy on the distributors business than they are a lopsided relationship will develop and you will become the leader of their group. There usually is a little disparity at first and that is fine, but your role is to be a resource and not the driving force of the distributors buisness. It is true that if you are putting in more than the distributor progress will be less efficient and success can be delayed. Your job is to create the right spirit and atmosphere where everyone can grow and succeed. You must also be very careful to make sure that you don't spend your time with people who are putting zero effort into the business. Simply ask yourself, "Do I want this for them more than they want it for themselves?" On the other hand, if the distributor is putting in the effort and time you are assured that you can invest your own time and energy into that person and be rewarded for your ability to build them into a productive distributor. Your goal as a leader is to create a peer or equal in the business by helping each distributor become the best they can be.

There are three phases of support. First, you work together as "one" with someone you have sponsored into the business. This new person brings to this "oneness" the assets of excitement and a circle of influence. Your assets as leader and supporter are knowledge, experience and success. You work directly with the new person to be the source of knowledge, experience and success that must be shared with a potential client or customer . The new person can bring in people they know and then you use your assets to give them the information they need to make a good decision.

The second phase is where you work together and are like oxen that are attached with a yoke. During this phase you will both contribute equally in meetings and discussions with interested people. As leader you will no longer dominate conversations or presentations but will support the distributor and be there as a resource for tough questions and as a model of success. This is where you truly use your abilities to transfer your knowledge and skills, through example, to the distributor. By working together in tandem you will begin to truly duplicate yourself and extend your abilities to the people in your network.

The third phase is where you separate and cooperate. As the individual builds their business and develops their knowledge, skills, experience and success there comes a time where they will become true equals with you. In fact they may even have a better understanding of some things than you do. This does not mean that you stop supporting them or that you aren't there to answer questions or give encouragement. It does mean that you respect them and recognize their insight is very valuable to you. You really develop a peer relationship with them which is exciting and fun. But, even if you have only been in the business a day longer you have more experience. With most distributors they will gain sufficient knowledge and skills to be successful. You as the leader however, have the opportunity to associate with many other people and you will gain vital insight and information that must be shared. You become a conduit of information and knowledge. New insight and knowledge is the greatest gift you can give a distributor. The more you duplicate yourself the more opportunities you have to share your experience and insight with individuals in the network.

As we have said, "raising a business is like raising a family" and there will be many similar challenges and frustrations. Some distributors will go through an "adolescence" stage. Any parent who has had a teenager knows the this is a tough stage to go through. When a distributor enters adolescence they can become a know-it-all and often try to go it alone. This usually results in frustration and failure and could even knock them out of the business. Even if the distributor seems to turn away from your support, encouragement and training, don't give up. Try to keep things positive and let them know that you are there for them. Eventually they will come around. We also see many leaders who try to hang on to long and don't cut the strings that will allow the distributor to spread his wings and grow. Don't let your ego get in the way and prevent someone else from reaching their full potential. Again, there is a fine line and a need to constantly evaluate your relationships and how you work with and support your people.

I will never forget the convention when we achieved our Blue Diamond status. We were really soaking it all in when Craig B. pulled us aside and said, "John and Giselle, you set the tone for the distributors in your network." It hit me like a ton of bricks; I had thought that I was coming to the convention to be in the spotlight and receive all the recognition and glory that I had worked for. I realized that a true leader and support person reflects the spotlight onto other people. I shifted my focus from absorbing the light to sharing it. I came to understand that I was at the convention to support my people, give them encouragement, spend time with them and help them feel that they were a vital part of the team. Sometimes you see a leader who is still in the adolescent stage of development. These leaders take all the light and recognition for themselves and let their ego become the driving force in their business. If they don't grow beyond this level they will be a shooting star instead of rising star in networking.

There are also three other facets to supporting your people. The first facet is to build excitement and a sense of belonging within each individual in your network. You can do this by sharing your enthusiasm for networking and relating your own experiences to the distributor. I will often do three way calls or go with a distributor to meet a new prospect, again to share my excitement and passion for the business and the products. The second facet of support is to praise the distributors success. Validate what they are doing well. Validating success produces greater results for the short-term and better performance down the line. You truly get what you validate. If a distributor did a great presentation or meeting, let them know about it! The third facet of support is to make sure that the distributor is doing the basics consistently. To succeed in this business you have to have many little successes day after day. It is like growing a plant; you can't just water it or give it sunshine occasionally or when it is convenient, you have to do it daily. Support your people by showing them what you do day in and day out to create the little successes.

Don't do things for your distributors that they can do for themselves. Many people think that support means doing almost everything for their people. This actually creates a distributor that can't do anything for himself. Developing in this business is like a chick hatching out of an egg. The chick gains strength and stamina through the effort of breaking out of the egg. If you step in and help the chick get out, it will not have the strength it needs to survive and the chick will soon die. Support but don't baby your distributors. A proper environment of support, enthusiasm and a sense of belonging attracts productive people and helps everyone become independent and successful leaders of their own networks.

Creating success in networking is contingent upon your ability to duplicate yourself and leverage your efforts with the efforts of others. We often call this the multiplier effect. If you rate your effectiveness from one to ten, you start out in the business as a one. What happens over time is that you develop your abilities and skills and go from being just one to being a 2,3,5, or 10 depending on experience, knowledge, enthusiasm, and financial success. As you increase your abilities and the abilities of those in your network, success starts to get exciting. For example, lets say that you get some knowledge, experience and productivity in the business and move your effective rate up to say a 5. Then you sponsor someone into your network that starts out as a 1 because they have little knowledge or experience. They also do not have a track record or a compelling story to tell of their success. This is where your support will help them become at least a 5 because you are there with them to share your experience, track record, and your story of success. Your efforts combined with theirs gives you 5x1=5. This may not seem too significant but 5 is definitely better than just 1x1=1. When you have 1x1 you have no growth and no opportunity for improvement or success. Now you nurture, raise, and train your new person and they develop a little track record and some financial success and become a 2 or a 3. 5x3=15. Then that person sponsors someone in the business who becomes a 2. Now you have 5x3x2=30. Now what if you grow to an 8 and the other two individuals become 5's? You have 8x5x5=200. You also have to be careful that you don't waste you time with someone who is not putting any effort into the business. You literally jump into a "black hole" that absorbs your energy and time when you continually work with someone who isn't committed to networking. If the individual isn't committed their effective rate is 0. Even if your are a 10 in your personal effective rate, 10x0=0. Find the people who are willing to make the effort and guide them all the way to success. It is vital that you stay with your people until they start multiplying themselves. There is a tendency to pull away too soon and you lose the multiplier effect and the chance to truly duplicate yourself. You may raise someone to a 7, leave too soon and suddenly they become a weak 7 and they only multiply 7x5=35. Stay with your people until you have successfully duplicated yourself. The multiplier effect is more than reason enough to raise your network right. *By training, supporting, and developing your people you can truly duplicate yourself and begin to naturally and dynamically extend yourself to unseen heights of achievement and success.*

John and Giselle:

It was New Years Eve and Diane and her 25 hair stylists were having a party to celebrate their success of the past year and look forward to an even better year to come. As the party wound down one of the stylists pulled Diane aside and said that he was leaving the company and about half of the staff was going with him to open their own salon. All of Diane's hard work was being pulled right out from under her. She had spent a great deal of time and money developing these people and now they were going to become her competition. In most traditional businesses this is the case, but in networking, if the compensation structure is right this won't happen. If you are dealing with a solid networking company you will be rewarded for your ability to develop the people you work with into leaders themselves. If you train them well they will be moving quality products to the end consumer in a productive manner and you will be compensated for your leadership. You do not create future competition by helping people succeed. You can only help yourself by helping others improve themselves in networking. Not only that, you are really compensated in proportion to the amount of leadership you give to your people. The more you give the more you receive. Can you imagine parents raising a child but not telling him or her everything for fear that they might become better than the parents? Of course not. A parent is going to share everything to assist a child in becoming the best possible person they can be. Networking works on the same principles. The principle is empowerment. You empower others to become their best and you will become your best.

As you can see, raising a successful network is very similar to raising a family. You need to have a foundation of values and principles that are rooted in high ethics and standards. Then you combine that with a solid work ethic, support, a nurturing attitude, and the multiplier effect and you have a winning combination that will empower your network to grow, thrive and succeed.

Total Commitment

John:

There are many ways to make a total commitment to this business, but far and away the best is to burn your bridges, don't look back and drive it forward. This is not a new concept. It is one that has been used by successful people throughout the ages. Many of the early explorers would actually burn their boats as they landed in a new land. This was there way of committing to make it or die. I am not saying that you have to be in a do or die mode with the business, but you do need to be in a position of urgency and importance if you want to succeed.

Until you make a total commitment, there is always hesitancy, that chance of retreating without having given it a good solid try. If you are always looking over your shoulder and wondering if you have made the right decision or whether you are spending your time on something worthwhile, you will never be able to succeed in this business. It is like plowing a field - if you are always looking back to where you have been, your rows will be crooked. If you focus on where you want to go, your rows will be long and straight. It is also true that if you are looking back and wondering, the dream stealers will have an easy time pulling you off track and preventing you from maximizing your efforts. Making a total and complete commitment will take you to the winners circle of success and achievement. The commitment you make is to become you. The best you can be will emerge as you make the commitment and take the responsibility for creating the life you desire.

Take time to evaluate you commitment to your business. How committed are you? Are you focusing on where you want to go or are you looking for possible escape routes back to the security of your old habits and attitudes? Making a commitment requires that you leave the confines of your comfort zone. Your comfort zone can become a prison that confines you and prevents you from living the life you would truly like to live. When we started in the business, I would never be the one to start a conversation, would never say "Hi" to someone I was sitting next to, and would never stand in front of a group to lead a discussion. I was always the one who would sit casually in the back of the room or back of the class and watch what others would do. In order to make it in this business, I had to make a commitment to overcome my comfort zone of sitting back and observing and force myself to interact with people. I know that if I can do it, you can do it. I was very shy and reserved which you would never know today. I had to burn my bridges on my comfort zone and get out there and make it happen.

Giselle:

Other comfort zones encountered by people in our business are current work status, fear of talking in front of groups and fear of selling anything. I qualified under all three.

I was in many ways very comfortable with what John had done in his manufacturing business and our lifestyle was good most of the time. As you remember from earlier chapters, I was less than thrilled when John decided to leave his business to start building his network. As we committed to networking I came to realize that commitment brings with it discomfort. I also have come to understand through our many experiences that discomfort accompanies growth.

Struggling through the process of discomfort and change is the cost of personal improvement. Personal growth is not found in by traveling the path of least resistance. You cannot grow and succeed without a solid commitment and a willingness to endure a few "growing pains." Hardly a day goes by that I don't talk to someone about their old job versus the opportunity of networking. I understand their reservations and concerns; and the thing that I always tell them is to go through the old Benjamin Franklin method of listing out the positives and negatives of each choice. In this business the positives always outweigh the negatives and it is just a matter of looking at the benefits and realizing that it is without a doubt the best way to reach their goals of freedom and happiness. When I have someone do this, they always seem to call back and say, "Giselle, I did what you suggested and I was very nervous. I now know that I need to move forward with my network and make a total commitment to it. Usually they do, and they enjoy some wonderful results.

I always had a fear of getting in front of others and presenting information. It took a long time for me to get comfortable and I still get a few butterflies before I go out to give a presentation. The thing that helped me the most was focusing on having fun. I also keep in my mind that they are just people and that they won't beat me up or throw things at me regardless of the quality of my presentation.

Presenting has actually become something that I enjoy doing now. It took a lot of time and a lot of focus, but I was committed to the business and knew that presenting was an important aspect.

You may also remember my fear of selling. This I had carried with me from my days as a Girl Scout. I always begged my family to buy the minimum amount so that I could wear my badge like the rest of the girls. Again, the thing to keep in mind is that it is not a do or die situation. If someone turns you down, it is not a big deal. All you have to do is move on to the next opportunity. We will discuss more about rejection in another chapter. Another key to selling is to have confidence in the product you are selling. This is easy in our organization because of the incredible quality in each and every product. You do have to use the product to be excited about the product and have the ability to persuade others to give it a try. It is like sharing with a friend your experience at a restaurant or movie; you only recommend what you know and like. Once you get into the product you can then enthusiastically talk about it to your friends, clients and potential clients.

Being committed is a necessary process that you must go through if you want to be able to succeed in the business of networking. Without it you have a lot of ups and downs, and probably more downs than ups. Total focus and commitment is what makes the difference between being a champion and an also ran in the race for success. Diffused light falls softly and has little to no impact on the object it hits. Intensely focused light on the other hand becomes a laser beam that can create a force powerful enough to cut through steel. Create your focus to cut through to a life of high achievement. Commit today to extend yourself through networking and be ready to experience some dramatic change, growth and achievement in your life as you begin to master yourself and your future.

The Abundance Mentality

Giselle:

After a great meeting I watched a little baby girl sitting at her mother's feet playing with a tambourine. She was really having a great time with the tambourine. Her enjoyment was observed by an older sibling who came over immediately and took the tambourine away. I expected to see some fighting and screaming between the young children and also anticipated the mother having an angry reaction to their behavior. To my surprise the little girl just moved on to the next toy and the mother continued her conversation. I later asked her why she hadn't interceded in the incident and how she had trained her little one to be content with another toy when the one he had been playing with was taken away. She replied, "Oh, there is always an abundance and you just have to move on to bigger and better things. It isn't what you have that makes you happy, it is what you do with what you have."

If only all of us could have that kind of abundance mentality. As we grow older we are programmed to hoard things and to try to get and hold on to as much as we can for as long as we can. If you want to succeed in this business you must have an abundance of an abundance mentality. The only way to succeed is by sharing what you have and what you know with others.

Nothing is of value to anyone until it is shared. Money has no worth or meaning until it is exchanged for something you want. Love is worthless until it is given away. The most beautiful scenery or painting is meaningless until it is shared and seen by others. The most brilliant ideas and thoughts are of no value until shared.

We have all seen how the miser of money is the most unhappy person in the world. We have seen that those who try to control others and maintain power seldom have success for long. It is like trying to hold water in your hand, the tighter you grip, the quicker it runs through your fingers.

One of the aspects of the business that I love the most is letting go of trade secrets and strategies for success. The focus in our network is to share these kinds of things as quickly as we can. We know that when others win we win too. There must be a free flow of information throughout your network if you want to keep it green and growing. Once you try to secure things for yourself and yourself alone, your network will begin to die on the vine. Share the wealth, share the information and reap the rewards of abundance.

John:

In many of our meetings I go into the audience and ask two or three people in the front row to tell me their names. They respond, "I am John or I am Jane Doe." I then tell them that is not really their name. They usually look at me a bit funny because they are sure that they are who they are! I then go on to tell them that their name is John or Jane Doe, President and CEO. They are the president and chief executive officer of their business. I like to think of it as ME, Inc. (ME, Inc. does not infer a self centered attitude. In fact I like to look at it as an acronym for More of Everything, More Enthusiasm, or Major Effort.) "ME, Inc." is a reflection of who you are and what you will do in the business of life. It is truly the most important company in the world.

One of the greatest aspects of networking is that there is room for a million Presidents and CEOs. Most traditional companies have room for only one, or occasionally two chief executives. In networking the key is to make everyone a president and a successful one. There is abundance in this business! The only question is who is going to work for it and who is going to reap the rewards of that hard work.

The other abundance is that you do not have to be a scholar or have any degrees to succeed in this business. It doesn't matter if you are shy, an extrovert, a psychologist, a farmer, or whatever. As long as you are willing to seek the abundance, you can accomplish almost anything you desire. I only have a 12th grade education and no special training to be in this business. I am not proud of or embarrassed by my education because I know that the abundance is there for me and everyone else regardless of education or background. I jokingly say that I have gained a working psychology degree because of all the people I have worked with, and thanks to networking and our finding the abundance, I now have an M.B.A. (Mega Bank Account!)

There are no boundaries, territories or divisions in the business of networking. You can contact anyone in any city in any country of the world. Your area is truly limitless. I get a little bit disgusted when I hear people say that there just aren't any good people in their area or that the area is really hard or even worse "saturated." I truly believe that there is no such thing as "saturated." The term is misunderstood and is usually only used by people who are making excuses for poor performance. The fact is that countless people thrive and succeed in a market that others call saturated!

The key here is what you are looking for. Are you focusing on the abundance or on the scarcity? Are you looking for opportunities or reasons to give up? There are wonderful people in every city in the world and there are a lot of them. You just have to take the approach that they are out there and your mission is to find them. I will give you a big hint on finding the abundance: "You will find what you are looking for!" If you are looking for opportunity, that is what you will find. If you are looking for scarcity, that is what you will find. If you are looking for good people you will find them and if you are looking for negative people you will find them, too. It is all in your attitude and mind set. Look inside to find yourself and the abundance of opportunities that exist to experience you! Seek the abundance and enjoy the fruit of abundance.

The Power of Being Positive

John:

Few things are as important as being positive in this business. Henry Ford was right when he said, "Whether you think you can or you think you can't, you are right!" High energy and excitement will take you a long way in networking because people are willing to stop, take notice, and listen to someone who is upbeat and positive about what they are doing.

Early on in our experience with networking I decided to run a few ads in Pennsylvania and see if I couldn't get some distributors going there. I also planned to spend some time looking for a voice mailbox to assist us in the business. I was able to stay at a friend's condominium for free so it seemed like a fairly safe bet. I was positive and ready for action even though it was a new area where I had no experience or contacts. The week went by and I had some incredible success with the ads. I met countless people and sponsored a significant number of new people into the business, but the best was yet to come.

As I was deciding what to do, I remembered that I wanted to check into a voice mail box for our incoming calls. I had been referred to several companies but they all came up blank. I was on my fourth contact and a little frustrated about the whole situation. I looked through the directory and called the business I was trying to contact. I spoke with the receptionist who asked a few questions about what I wanted and then she said, "Oh, you must talk with our Vice President of Sales." I was transferred and began speaking with a fellow named Scott. For the first 10 minutes we were both talking a hundred miles an hour. I was excited and he was excited but we were talking about two completely different things. He thought I was interested in buying a $25,000 voice mail system when I was excited about getting a $25 a month voice mail box.

Scott then asked me why I needed the voice mail and what I was doing in Philadelphia. I explained that I was opening up a new area for an exciting business. I also told him that I had left my own business and was now pursuing this opportunity full time. It was a Monday morning and Scott could not believe that anyone could possibly be that positive about work. Scott was having a typical Monday wishing he could get out of his business and reflecting on the fact that most heart attacks occur on negative and depressing Monday mornings at work. My enthusiasm and excitement caught his attention and he was very interested. I then said, "Scott, wouldn't it be funny if someday soon we were both making incredible money and were walking the beaches of the world together with our families?" He dropped the phone. Picking it back up he said, "Excuse me, but what did you say?" I very enthusiastically repeated what I had said before and then set up a time to get together. Soon after our meeting Scott signed into the business and started making things happen. Eight months later his wife Nancy signed in and they became a dynamic duo. Today, Scott and Nancy are one of the organization's most successful teams and they are literally making all the money they desire and are walking the beaches of the world with their family. In fact, just recently Giselle and I went on an incredible cruise to Greece with Scott and Nancy and laughed our way along the coastal beaches as we relived our initial meeting. As Scott reflects back on this initial, chance meeting, he often says that the only reason that he didn't just hang up on me was because I was so excited about what I was doing. My being excited not only helped Scott and Nancy get where they wanted to go but also helped Giselle and me get where we wanted to go. There is no substitute for being positive.

Giselle:

Being positive also helps you maintain your sanity and assists you in overcoming adversity. Being positive is a habit just like brushing your teeth or driving to work. It is something you develop and improve over time by practice and repetition.

Craig T. gave us a wonderful opportunity to stay in his gorgeous condominium in Park City, Utah. The setting was a beautiful slope at a wonderful ski resort. We arrived on the 10th of December so we could enjoy the snow and fun with the kids for two weeks and truly experience a white Christmas. (White Christmases are rare in Florida.)

I shipped all of the Christmas presents out early and had them locked up in the laundry room on the lower level of the condominium. After our arrival the kids skied every day thoroughly enjoying themselves. Everything was going great! Then our wonderful white Christmas began to unravel. On the Friday before Christmas, John was out skiing and had a terrible accident. We went to the doctor and found out that John needed to have major surgery on his knee. Early Saturday morning I awakened to a phone call from Florida. Our home had been broken into and most everything of value had been stolen. All of our TVs and VCRs, all of our nice things were gone. I tried to tell Angelo, who was watching the house, that everything was fine and that I was glad that he wasn't there when it happened. I assured him that everything was replaceable and there was nothing to worry about.

Monday came and we were busily getting everything ready for Christmas Eve dinner. The weather had turned cold, much colder. In fact, I believe that it was the coldest Christmas Eve in 100 years. We had some problems with the spa outside so a serviceman had come to fix it. He had opened a few of the valves and the pipes were frozen. He said as he left that he would be back the day after Christmas to make sure that everything was all right. I went back to getting things ready. The kids were antsy and John was a little bit down as he thought about the surgery scheduled the day after Christmas. I went down stairs to do a load of wash and upon opening the door I saw small pond of floating presents. The serviceman had left the valve open, the pipe thawed and water and presents were running everywhere.

My heart sank; it was 5:00 p.m. on Christmas Eve and all of our presents were soaking wet. I didn't know what to do. I waited until the kids were in bed and began the task of unwrapping all of the gifts, drying them as best I could and then rewrapping them one by one. It was a long night. The next morning as the kids opened their gifts they asked why everything was damp and wet. I said, "It was snowing last night and I am sure that Santa got a little bit of snow on the presents before he delivered them. We survived the morning.

That afternoon I called Richard K. who is one of our up-line support people to wish him a Happy Holiday. As I shared with him everything that had happened over the previous few days, I was laughing and giggling as I described how we went from one catastrophe to the next. He stopped me and said, "Giselle, how can you be laughing? Your husband is going in for major surgery in the morning, your home has been broken into and everything stolen, and your Christmas got washed away in a flood! You are amazing, Giselle, I don't know how you do it."

I thought about it for a minute and then said, "You know, Richard, if I were watching the events that happened to us over the last few days at a movie theater I would be rolling in the aisles. Why not keep a positive focus and enjoy all that we do have right now. Laughter really is the best medicine, and who knows, maybe I can write it down and sell it to Chevy Chase for his next vacation movie!"

To me, attitude is everything, especially in this business. If you are positive when things are going right and even when things are going wrong, you can make it big in this business. When you are positive, the world will step aside and watch as you race toward your goals. Keep positive and focused and you can make a difference in the lives of others and create a truly dynamic network.

John and Giselle:

These are just two examples of what being positive has done for us. There are countless times that our ability to stay positive has helped us in our business and in our relationships with others. As we have said before, being positive is a habit. It is something that you can learn and develop. Strive to build your "positive muscles" and we are certain you will see a difference in all aspects of your life. Reflect and learn from each experience. Develop your ability to adapt and change and then take new action to improve and develop you.

The Time of Our Lives

John and Giselle:

One of the most precious commodities in the whole world is time. Time is what life is made of. Many a ruler has uttered the words, "My kingdom for another moment of time." We have learned many things about time over the last seven years and would like to share a few insights with you.

One of the examples we often use in our training is that of a bank account. If you had a bank account that credited you

$86,400 at the beginning of each day and allowed you to keep no cash in it and would cancel whatever portion you had failed to use each evening, what would you do? The obvious answer of course is to draw out every cent every day.

Each of us have such a bank account, and it is called "time." Every single morning of your life you are credited with 86,400 seconds. Every evening that "time" which you have not used or wasted is cancelled from your account never to be returned. Your "time" account carries no balances forward and does not allow any overdrafts. There is no chance to draw on tomorrow's deposit and there is no storing the time you have wasted.

When you look at time as a bank account, your time does become your most precious asset. There are a lot of myths about time and how we spend it. We often hear distributors who are struggling say, "I just don't have the time to make my business work." The truth is that they are just not focusing their time in such a way that allows them to use it on their network. It is amazing to us that people will say that they don't have time to do things, but will talk to you for an hour about nothing, watch television for several hours a night or take two hours to go out to lunch. If they would limit a few of these activities they would have more than enough time to make their business successful. You simply have to choose how you are going to spend your time. Keep in mind that if you take care of the minutes, the days, months and years will take care of themselves.

We have found that one of the greatest aspects of the business of networking is that it gives you more time. By running our business out of our home we figure we save at least one to two hours per day of driving time. It also allows us the luxury of being with our children and to have more quality and quantity time with them. We also have more time for vacations and family outings. To do this we created some priorities. Priorities allow you to spend time doing that which will move you a step closer to your goals.

We know a lot of people who are very busy. They always seem to be running somewhere, always in a hurry, always behind schedule. It is critical that you make a distinction between being busy and being productive. You can fill your days with all kinds of activities but not move closer to your goals. We believe that activity without accomplishment equals delusion and activity with accomplishment equals production. This is where prioritizing comes in. You only have so many minutes and seconds in the day to use on your priorities. Picture it like a checker board with each block representing an hour of your day. Which activities are most important to your success right now? Make a move and get going on that activity, Now! Don't wait another second. It is amazing what you can get done once things are properly prioritized. Being able to prioritize is one of the necessities of this business.

You must have strong self discipline to be self-employed. Too many people think that being self-employed is easy and a very casual lifestyle. The truth is that it takes twice, if not more, the discipline to work for yourself than it does to work for someone else. You have to be able to say "no" to extra sleeping time and "yes" to getting up and getting going. No supervisor is going to make sure you get started on time. You must be able to say "no" to flipping on the television and "yes" to making the first call of the day. One of the best ways to evaluate your self-discipline is to hold yourself accountable and keep score of your performance. In your planning make sure that you take the time to write down how many appointments, meetings, training sessions and follow-up calls you had for the day and for the week. These statistics will give you a very clear picture of how you are doing and if you have the discipline it takes to be self-employed. It is true that most millionaires in the world are self-employed; and it is also true that most of them have the self-discipline to prioritize.

Another aspect of prioritizing your time and activities is the time spent with each of the distributors in your network. To truly become productive you must be the catalyst to help people become productive. You have to take the belief and desire that a new distributor possesses and get them to take action. Belief without action kills belief. If a new person in the business has high belief in networking but takes no action they will soon lower their belief to match their unproductive behavior. You must build a strategy for each new person to give them opportunity to take action that will validate their belief.

When I find someone who is only marginally productive, I will contact them and talk to them as if they were a new prospect. I will focus the call on building a stronger relationship with them. I will ask them how the products are working for them and if there is anything I can do to be of service to them. Spend time finding and developing the individuals who are going to become an eight, nine, or ten. These will become true leaders in your network. I think the real deciding factor on whether or not to invest time with someone is their <u>commitment</u>.

Another killer of time, action, motivation, and many networking individuals is confusion. When we are confused, we are not in a position to work effectively or productively. Many people leave the business because they get confused and unsure of what they should do and so they do nothing, get frustrated and throw away the dream. New people in the business, in particular, need a clear focus with a definite plan and a set of specific priority action steps.

The first and foremost priority in networking is to sell the products and sponsor new people into the network. There is nothing more important! It is the lifeblood of your business. The second priority is to spend time training and developing people. The third area of priority is dealing with challenges and the fourth is to delegate additional work. Another way to look at your priorities is that if you were only going to get one thing done in your day, what would you chose to do? Another question to ask yourself is, "Why am I doing this activity and what results will it produce?" We have also found that if the "why" is big enough the "how" is usually pretty easy. Create a reason for what you are doing. Make sure that it is in harmony with your mission and your long-range goals.

It is also vital to keep in mind that productivity begins with you. No one else is accountable for your production. It is a mistake to think that others are responsible for your productivity. By putting the load of responsibility on others, you are giving away your power to succeed and may be throwing away your opportunity. When you take things into your own hands, you remove a lot of the frustration that comes from assuming that your success is controlled by someone else.

Giselle:

I have long felt that there has been a need for a special time management course for mothers. Mothers are always on call and have so many interruptions during their day that it is easy to feel overwhelmed and under accomplished. For me, planning has been a vital ingredient. I plan to do certain activities during specific times of the day; then I know I have a very good chance of getting them done. I try to do a lot of odd jobs in the morning while the children are getting ready for school. I know that I will be interrupted a lot during this time with things like; "Mom, I need help with this. Mom, I can't find my homework. Mom, have you seen my shoes. Mom, I need this shirt ironed." I am sure you are familiar with the routine. Having a lot of little projects to work on during this time of day works out great for me. Too often I think we don't start things because we only have 10 to 15 minutes to work before we have to leave or take the kids somewhere. I have found that by capturing this little time with little projects I can get a lot accomplished before the children leave for school.

I plan my major activities or important phone calls around the time that my youngest will take a nap. Now this can vary from day to day but I do know a general block of time where it is likely that he will go down for a rest. I also use the time when the children are working on their homework as a time for me to do some of my homework too. It makes the children get into their studies when they know that I am at the table with them working on my own things. It also allows me to answer their questions and help them with their problems.

There are many demands on mothers, especially single mothers. I am fortunate to have a wonderful husband who takes a lot of his time to assist me with the children and things around the house. I think one of the keys, again, is prioritizing. Sometimes it might be more important for you to work on your network than it is to vacuum the stairs; and sometimes it is more important that you read with your children than it is to work on your business or clean a room. I am a firm believer in "Mother knows best!" Trust your instincts and prioritize your way to success.

You must also have a solid perspective on your success. Too often we compare apples to oranges instead of apples to apples. If you are working the business part time and spending 10 hours a week developing your network, you cannot compare your success to someone who is spending 50 hours a week. You also can't compare it to a couple that is spending 50 hours each on the business. The only thing you can compare is the effectiveness of the time you have put in. This again comes back to the fact that you must prioritize if you want to maximize your efforts. Networking is like golfing in that you really should compete against yourself and the course as opposed to competing against individuals. You are out there competing against your previous best score and striving to improve you performance based on your efforts. Look at your best months in terms of production and effectiveness then create a game plan to better that effort by working smarter as well as harder.

John:

I think there are a lot of little things that you can do to use your time for the accomplishment of your goals. One thing that is a must for me is to always have a project to work on when I am waiting in an airport or waiting for an appointment. It is amazing how much you can accomplish while you are sitting and waiting for someone else.

I also like to stay out in front of projects and objectives. There is nothing worse than to come down to the wire on a project and run out of time. I estimate how long activities are going to take so that I can allow adequate time for their completion.

Writing things down is a challenge for me because I am usually totally focused on the task at hand. I agree, however, that writing things down helps you to relax a little bit and move projects forward in an organized way. A lot of people get very stressed out because they are trying to remember all of the things that they need to do. They carry all of their "to dos" around with them all day in their minds. When your mind is racing from one project to the next and then back to the first one, you need to stop and write a few things down.

Planning each week the week before and planning each day the day before is a great way to maximize your time. We are often caught in a reactive position when we haven't created a game plan for the day and week. When someone calls and asks you to do something, if you don't have a plan you usually just react and say, "Oh sure, no problem, I'll get it done." Usually you wish you hadn't said that because you really didn't have time to do what you agreed to do. On the other hand, if you do have a game plan for the day and that same request comes in, you are empowered to respond and say either, "Yes, I can see that this is important and I will take care of it right now." or you can politely say, "I am working on another priority right now, can I get back with you this afternoon or first thing tomorrow?" Planning puts you in control of your time and your life.

People who say they have a time management problem are really just experiencing a lack of focus and direction. If you feel swamped and overwhelmed with what you have to do, take a few moments and review your goals. Are you doing things that lead toward or away from your goals? Create action plans that take you where you really want to be. Use a planner to prioritize your days and weeks. Now, when I say use a planner, I mean that the things you write down are the things you do. Too often we write a million things down in a planner and then we just react to everything else that happens during the day and spend our time on low priorities. Look at your list often and make sure that you are working only on what you wrote down as a priority.

By creating meaningful priorities you can really begin to maximize every hour of every day. When you use your time wisely you can experience meaningful personal time, private time, family time and become the true you. Time is an equal opportunity employer and gives each person the same amount of time as the next. It is a level playing field where those who guard and use time effectively are rewarded with the time of their lives.

Procrastination Carries out the Assassination of Motivation

John and Giselle:

One of our themes over the last seven years has been, "Take Action Now!" If everyone in the networking business would give strict heed to this motto, we would all be a lot better off and would be enjoying much more of what life has to offer. Procrastination kills motivation, it paralyzes people and dashes dreams.

I am sure you have seen this scenario and perhaps experienced it yourself. An individual attends an opportunity or training meeting and is very, very motivated to improve himself and increase his business. He returns home committed to a higher level of performance. He arrives home around nine or ten to find a few messages on the answering machine from some prospects or down-line associates. "What a tremendous meeting," he thinks to himself as he sets the messages aside to deal with tomorrow. No sense getting involved with anything right now. "Let me see, I should focus on my action plan for tomorrow and review what I learned at the meeting so I can put it into my long term memory. Well, I really do need some time to relax, after all I have earned it by working all day and night." He then hits the sofa and is quickly mesmerized by TV images and the assassination of motivation is well under way.

His morning gets off to a rather slow start having slept in after catching the end of one more rerun of "The Love Boat." By now the excitement of the previous night's training meeting is almost a dream; and he may not even be able to remember the wonderful information and action plans to improve his business. One glance at the phone messages from the previous night and they are set aside until afternoon when he will be fully awake. Next, goals and action plans. "Well, this prospect is probably busy right now anyway and, well, he wasn't really that interested either. I could learn about some of the new products but I should probably wait until later when I won't get interrupted by a phone call. I could check to see what is happening with some of the new people who have signed up in my down-line, but they might have a problem or a question and I don't want to deal with it right now." The story goes on and on with the big question remaining: "Why isn't my network growing and succeeding for me?" Remember that your actions must match your beliefs. If there is no action your belief will drop, doubts will rise and procrastination will destroy your goals and dreams.

Procrastination is the most lethal killer in networking. We have seen scores of people give in to its powers and promises of a better day tomorrow. Procrastination is the right arm of the dream stealers. It helps them by knocking down your self esteem each time you put off an important task. Inactivity breeds inactivity. In the same fashion, success breeds success and ability begets more ability. The more you do, the more you will want to do; and the less you do the less likely you will ever do anything at all. Don't let procrastination assassinate your motivation. Take action now!

Challenges and Opportunities

John and Giselle:

Challenges and obstacles are really opportunities to evaluate where you are and where you want to go in the future. When challenges arise you need to view them as corrective feed back and a chance to take your performance to a higher level.

Not long after we decided to go with networking full time, some very interesting things started to take place. The first thing was a sudden decrease in our income. Then, despite bringing significantly more people into our organization, our income did not increase in proportion to our efforts. We were totally committed to make the business work. There was absolutely no way we were going back. In fact the thoughts of going back really scared us. We didn't want to go back, only forward and upward. We reflected on what we refer to as, "If we both don't give up on the same day we will make it" era. When setbacks and challenges occur it is very natural to have a desire to quit and go back to a previous comfort zone. Early on it was interesting to note that on the days John was down, Giselle was up and on the days that Giselle was down, John was up. This was fortunate because had we both been down on a particular day, we may have thrown away our dream and returned to a life that could not have satisfied either one of us. By staying focused we were able to turn the challenge into a positive way of life that has taken us to many peak experiences.

We feel that it is a law of nature that when you choose to truly commit to something, almost immediately there is an intense storm of opposition, setbacks and challenges. It is almost as if the universe is testing you to see if you are really committed or if you are just kind of moving along and waiting to see what happens. It is only by total commitment that you can make it in this business, or any business for that matter.

The most important thing is to keep focused on the positive when the challenges arise. You must keep a proper mind set and worry only about those things over which you have control. We spend too much time and energy worrying about things that we simply cannot control. Things like the weather, the government, other people, and so on are things that we cannot control directly. It is very easy to become obsessed with what others are doing and the fact that it may or may not be affecting your business or your family. Your mind becomes preoccupied and cannot zero in on what you need to do to succeed. You end up making excuses for your failures and blame your lack of success on something else.

You must take responsibility for yourself and your network. Do all that is within your ability to change and improve and move toward your goals. Give no attention to sayings like: "The government or the economy is killing my business." "This is a bad time of year to do business." "If only my up-line or down-line would get it together then I can make this work." All of these attitudes place responsibility on someone or something else. It is interesting to look at the past and see that regardless of external circumstances, people in all ages have had tremendous success, made fortunes and achieved greatness.

There are a lot of things in this business and in life that we simply cannot control. You cannot control your age or your gender, but you can control what happens to you. You can control your diet and exercise, which has a lot to do with how you look in relationship to those passing years. You really have to begin focusing on the things over which you do have control. One lady kept complaining about the people in her area and the difficult circumstances she was encountering. She complained for a long time. She then realized that every time she didn't want to take action and do something positive she would go to the refrigerator and get something to eat. She was gaining weight and sinking her business. One day, as she opened her refrigerator for another "avoidance" snack, she said to herself, "This is not the door to success!" She slammed the door and went right to the phone and began making the contacts that would lead her to the life she wanted. She was taking control and responsibility for a challenging situation.

One of the greatest aspects of this business is the ability to thrive in any country under almost any social or economic condition as long as there are people who believe in the concept and the product and are willing to work to make it happen. There is no get rich quick philosophy inherent in networking. There are some companies that will promote and instill "get rich quick" in their people, but such companies are usually not around very long. Focus on what you can do instead of what you can't do and you will thrive under practically any circumstance.

One challenge that everyone in the business of networking encounters is a "cold market." When you start in the business, you focus on your "warm market," which consists of your friends, family, acquaintances, associates and so forth. These people are much easier to approach because you have already established a relationship of trust. At some point you will have to branch out and begin contacting people you do not know or people with whom you have no relationship. This is the "cold market." There are a few ways to work through and keep your momentum going after you have gone through your "warm market." One of the best ways is to always seek and obtain referrals. Referrals can keep you in a warm market for a long time. Another thing to keep in mind is that when people say "no," it may just be a matter of timing and they may be ready a few weeks or months from now. Rather than getting upset with this challenge, simply respond by saying, "That isn't a problem, I will get back with you in a little while with an update of what is happening." When you get into the colder markets, begin by creating a curiosity that will cause the individual to give you the time you need to present the information about the business. Then give them just enough information to get them moving in the right direction. Don't give them a drink with a fire hose. Develop a good relationship with the individual. When you are viewed as a friend and trusted person your success rate will increase dramatically. In some cases it is best to develop that strong relationship before you ever ask them to make a decision. Take a personal interest in them and what they are doing. True, it will be a challenge for you, but it is a challenge that countless people have turned into the greatest opportunity of a lifetime.

Our parent company is another wonderful example of using challenges and setbacks as opportunities. After several years of tremendous company growth and success the media went on a rampage of negative stories, most of which were totally unfounded. Most companies would have simply bashed back or folded under the pressure and scrutiny. In other companies facing this challenge, many distributors leave and the overall network is substantially weakened. Our company, on the other hand, chose to take swift action to meet with everyone concerned and spent thousands of dollars looking at possible problems and establishing mini-networks to combat the challenges. At the same time the company was in constant communication with leaders and distributors sharing any and all new information and input as soon as it was available. Instead of having people leaving in hoards, our networks actually became more united and the commitment became even stronger to the company and to its people. Some distributors left and some returned, and those that didn't return stand in awe of the resilience of the company and the solidarity of the distributors. Most companies would have gone into a conservative mode but our company went into expansion, spending large sums of money on new products, communication, public relations and support. Our company rose higher and reached farther than ever before. Many interesting alliances developed as a result of these set backs. The company was able to work directly with government officials in almost every state and also with the federal government. Attitudes were changed, misperceptions erased and common ground established. A challenge that would have wiped out many companies served only to strengthen and improve ours. In fact our parent company is now the standard and the measuring stick by which all other network companies are compared. Improvement is what taking advantage of challenges is all about.

This challenge also proved another important point - word of mouth is stronger than the media. Many people thought that the organization's distributors would exit in droves as a result of the negative media blitz. What happened was the distributors became even more united because they were given the right information from headquarters. There also a commitment by the distributors to product quality. We all knew that great results come from using the product so we were able to withstand the challenge and strengthen ourselves as a result. (Remember that word of mouth is by far the best way to build your network!)

Craig T. assisted us by giving a training session in Miami one evening, and we all felt that it went fantastic. We were standing near the front of the room at the conclusion when a man came up to Craig and starting raking him over the coals. The man was incredibly upset and was complaining about his up-line and down-line, the parent company and just about everyone else. It would have been very easy for Craig to become angry and defensive in response to the verbal attack he faced, but he chose to turn the challenge into an opportunity. Craig expressed to the gentleman that it was not wise to think that he needed or even could control his up and down line or the company. Craig discussed the importance of controlling your own attitude and actions and being responsible for your own success. After several minutes the man began to see the light. He realized that all of the challenges and situations he was angry about were just opportunities to improve himself and his network. Today he is a Blue Diamond executive and enjoying a wealth of success and freedom.

It would have been easy with any challenge or situation we have described to pout and complain and say, "That isn't fair!" We chose to focus on what we could do to turn the negative into a positive. That is what you need to do with every aspect of your business and personal life. There is a Chinese proverb that says crisis is opportunity riding a dangerous wind. When you face challenges, obstacles, and crisis, be sure to focus on that which you can control, don't worry about that which is beyond your power and you will make your goals and dreams a reality.

Rejuvenating With Rejection

John:

Without fail, rejection is the one thing that every distributor will encounter in networking. It is truly part of the business. Rejection comes from a variety of sources - friends and family, business associates and total strangers. In order to survive in the business, you must understand rejection and learn what you can do to turn it into a positive.

Giselle:

When we started in the business, rejection was without a doubt my greatest fear and concern. I wasn't equipped with the mind set and tools to deal with rejection. I would be very hurt when someone would say "no" to the products or the business opportunity. I felt very vulnerable and unprepared to take rejection and turn it into something good or to just let it slide off my back.

In training meeting I attended Carol K. shared a metaphor that proved very helpful. She had watched how the waitress in a restaurant would go from table to table asking if anyone would care for more coffee. Nine times out of ten the waitress was told "no", rejected from her purpose and offer. Yet, she kept on doing it. Table after table she would ask and usually be rejected and just keep going about her business. She did not go crying to her manager that it wasn't fair or that no one was accepting what she had to offer. She kept at it and provided great service to every customer.

If you can approach networking in the same way as a waitress, you should be able to find much success. Remember also that people are not rejecting you as an individual, they are simply not at the right place in their lives to look at and appreciate the dynamics of the opportunity. It has nothing to do with your own personal value or self-worth. When I go out to talk with new people I like to think that I put on a special suit. This suit protects my insides from any rejection or hurt that someone may try to inflict. Then, if I am rejected, it simply bounces off of my suit and the inner me is not affected at all.

Out of the blue one day I received a call from a lady named Lucia who had just moved into the area. She had enrolled her children in the same school as my kids and had obtained my name and number from the principal. She mentioned to the principal that she had been involved with the Better Baby Institute and the principal replied, "Then you must know Giselle Sexsmith, because Giselle is deeply committed to the principles of the institute." Lucia called and was very excited to find someone else who was teaching their children based on the Institute's philosophy. We decided to get together and take our kids to the beach. We had a wonderful time talking and visiting. I had several of our products in my bag and began putting some on as we talked. She asked me about them and wanted to give them a try. She did, loved the results and signed on as a distributor mostly so she could use the product. A few weeks later she called and said that her husband was interested in hearing about the business because he had seen the results the products were giving his wife. I went over to their house where we had coffee, chatted for a while and then moved into the living room to talk about the business. I must admit that I was intimidated as I sat across from Jim. You see Jim is about 6'6", very strong, has a black belt in judo, is a graduate from Yale and has an MBA. I was 5'2", 100 lbs., and spoke with an accent. I gave it my best shot by giving him my entire presentation for over 45 minutes. As soon as I stopped speaking, he said, "If you can find someone who understands this business and can explain it to me, I will listen." This was a major rejection! I had given him my all. As I drove home I could really feel the rejection that was in his words, even if he didn't mean it. This could have knocked me out, but instead I got home and immediately put John in contact with Jim. Then I got Jim to meet Jerry and some of the other leaders in the network. It wasn't long before Jim and Lucia were both full scale into the business and now they are Blue Diamond Executives. You have to bounce back after rejection and find new ways to move forward toward you goal. If I had let the initial rejection pull me down I would have missed the opportunity to have two dynamite people in our network.

I think that the fear of rejection is by far the greatest fear we face in life. The thought of being rejected by a friend or loved one is even worse and almost unthinkable. This causes many people to not share their business with those they love. The way I look at it is that it would be much more painful if a loved one came to me and saw my freedom and success and said, "Why didn't you share this with me? Why didn't you tell me about this opportunity?" Can you even imagine the pain that would cause you? You definitely need to look beyond the immediate possibility of rejection and begin serving everyone around you.

John:

Another way to look at rejection is as a stepping stone toward success. If you can calculate how many people you need to talk to in order to enroll one new person into your network and then calculate what that one new person will mean as an asset to your network, you can create a meaningful equation. You can figure out approximately what you are getting paid for each rejection. That way, you are in essence getting paid for every activity you perform regardless of the outcome.

It is critical that you assist your distributors in dealing with rejection, especially when they are new in the business. New distributors go through an initial stage that I call the "Wide Awake" stage. This is a time when they stay up all night thinking about how they are going to spend their money and time with the freedom they will create. Often this sets people up for failure. It is important that you tell your new distributors that there will be potholes and problems, setbacks and many rejection, including some from people they love. You have to tell them the truth. Otherwise, when they hit that rejection, they blame you for not telling them it would happen and they may even throw away their dream. By sharing the realities of rejection with them, they will become much more teachable in the way to succeed in the business. They will come to value your opinions and instruction more because you were honest and open with them from the start.

I will often go with a new distributor on his first several calls. It helps them to feel more confident knowing they have someone there to answer any of the real tough questions. It is true that knowledge and enthusiasm lead to effectiveness and productivity. Going with a new distributor gives me the opportunity to share and transfer much of my knowledge and enthusiasm. The most important reason for going, however, is to absorb the rejection for them if the appointment doesn't turn out quite right. I can take the heat and some of the negative feelings away from them. This helps new distributors stay positive, upbeat and on track for their future success. This process is really one of the best forms of training and ensuring another's success in the business.

I think that it is also important that you help your new distributors use the best possible methods to create their network. There is a form of "silent" rejection that takes place when you are training a new distributor. The new distributor may have some wild and crazy ideas for succeeding in the business. We have found that it is best to use the tested methods first to build your confidence and approach before you venture out into the new methods. Too many leaders don't say anything when a new distributor announces, "I am going to try this new idea of mine and it is going to change the business." If you remain silent you may be sending a message of approval to the new distributor. If their new idea doesn't work they will then look to you and ask why you didn't prepare them for the rejection and failure or help them avoid it all together. Don't give up your role as leader. Help your new people use the established methods in the beginning to gain the confidence they need to expand and better succeed down the road.

You almost have to think like a robot when it comes to rejection. How many calls would you do and how many rejections would you take if you were a robot? Robots don't have feelings like we do; they don't get tired and they keep moving and accomplishing their purpose until they are shut down. If you can learn to let the rejection slide past you and just keep moving forward like a robot, you will be on a path to success in networking.

It is very wise to take a look at each rejection and success shortly after it takes place. Evaluate your performance and determine what you did good and what you did poorly. You can then create a game plan to help you improve for your next opportunity. Remember again, failure is only corrective feedback and will reveal itself until you change your patterns for success.

You must feel that you have an important message to share and that what you know will indeed help others, but it is up to them to act on it. Suppose you found out that a terrible hurricane was coming and it would start destroying your town in just two short hours. You would definitely have a responsibility to share that information with as many people as you could. Once you have told someone, it is then up to that person to use or not use the information to his advantage. In the business of networking you do have a valuable message that needs to be shared. Once you have shared it, however, it is then up to the individual to evaluate whether or not they will use it to enjoy success and freedom. If they reject it, they have rejected the message and not you!

There are really only three reasons why someone might reject the opportunity to get involved in networking. The first two are legitimate and the third is a little bit tongue in cheek. The reasons are: 1. You didn't do your job right and they haven't understood; 2. The timing simply is not right for them to get into the business; and 3. They are a little loony and you really don't want them in your network anyway. We will look at the first two and leave number three up to your judgment. Again, the first reason is that they don't understand it or you haven't explained it to them correctly or with the right energy. This first rejection is the corrective feedback kind. Use this kind of rejection to evaluate your performance and improve your techniques and enthusiasm. The second reason they might reject the opportunity is timing. There is not much you can do about this rejection, but you can set yourself up for the moment when the time is right by being positive and telling them that you will keep them posted on what is happening. All rejections can be turned into a rejuvenating process providing you look at each in the correct light and use all of them as tools to improve yourself.

High Tech
and
High Touch

Giselle:

I mentioned earlier in the book that a real turning point for me was hearing Clara say that running a networking business was like raising a family. I found this to be most comforting and encouraging. I have been comforted and continually amazed at all of the high tech features of our business that allow us to operate around the world with tremendous ease. The computer systems, accounting procedures, shipping ability and more truly make networking a high tech business. Sometimes, though, I feel that many of us lose sight of the high touch aspect which is even more vital to your success than high tech.

It is nice to have all of your accounting and shipping done without even having to lift a finger, but it is more important to touch the hearts of your people and build them as you build your business. I often equate what we are doing to Walt Disney. He was a master of high tech and high touch. He used some of the greatest minds in the world as his "Imagineers" and created technical processes that were light years ahead of the world. Then he added his most important ingredient - heart touching. In everything he did, from animated movies to rides and theme parks, his use of high tech was always to augment his high touch of individual lives. No one ever left a Disney movie or a day at Disney Land without feeling a little bit better about themselves and the world around them. That is what networking is all about.

As you work with your people make sure that you don't allow the high tech of voice mail and fax machines to ever rob you of the benefits of high touch activities. You truly need to become personally interested in the lives of all of your people. This is not a surface commitment but a deep and profound determination to make a difference in someone's life. It is not always easy but it is always worth while. Take time to make note of special occasions or accomplishments. A phone call or letter can have a profound effect on an individual. Just knowing that someone is concerned and interested in them can really make a difference for most people. Use this high touch to solidify your network and to surround yourself with a circle of friends that will last a lifetime.

John:

Every time we eat out, I think about the tradition of paying a tip at the end of the meal to the waiter or waitress. This tradition has been modified and changed over the years, and I wonder which is the better approach. It use to be that a tip was paid before the meal to ensure the best kind of service. I think that this philosophy applies directly to networking.

I often say that we need to appreciate in advance. We need to appreciate before anything is done so that people know that we are concerned for them regardless of their performance. It is very easy to fall into a reward based system of praise and appreciation. Just like with our children, it is always easy to tell them how wonderful they are or how much we love them after they have done something good. Sometimes it is difficult to do so when things aren't going so smoothly. The message this sends to our children is that our love and appreciation for them is dependent upon their performance. This is the wrong message! The happiest and best adjusted children are those who know they are loved unconditionally by their parents. They do not have to worry if they happen to strike out, lose the game, hit a wrong note or make a mistake. They can focus on the positive things they want to do and not look over their shoulder to see if failure is sneaking up on them. When children are appreciated in advance, they are more likely to succeed.

The individuals in your network are the same. They need to be appreciated in advance in order to perform their best. If they are only appreciated when they have a banner month, they are instilled with a mind set that I must perform to be of any worth. Some people may perform well for a while under such a system but they will fail miserably in the long run. They really need to know that your interest in them is unconditional and that you are truly concerned about them as an individual. This is high touch.

Random reinforcement is also an important part of giving appreciation in advance. If people think that they are only going to receive praise at certain times or events, they tend to discount its value and worth. If you are random in giving praise and reinforcement at various times, it comes across much more sincere and personal. Keep tabs on your people and their families because there are countless opportunities to solidify relationships with positive reinforcement and meaningful praise.

The men and women who fight forest fires are a special group that understand high tech and high touch. In many cases they will have to parachute into a remote location to battle a fire. Timing is critical for those who jump from the plane amid the smoke and wind that go along with these kind of blazes. If they jump too soon they will land in the fire and encounter serious injury or even death. If they jump too late they will land too far away and will be unable to assist in fighting the blaze. Because of this they depend greatly on sensitive equipment and precision planning. Yet, even with all of the high tech equipment they have on board from navigational instruments to gauges and intricate maps and forecasts, when it comes to jumping out of the plane at the precise moment they rely on a soft "touch." The jumpers will line up along the open cargo door and the leader will lay down behind them and give each jumper a light touch on the leg when they are to leap from the aircraft. The jumpers don't trust their ears or even the high tech lights and sirens that signal the time jump. The do, however, trust their leader and know that he is totally committed to their success and safety. A simple touch is more reassuring than any high tech device. With the individuals you work with make sure that you show them that you are a leader who is committed assist them in reaching success quickly and safely. As the leader you have a moral obligation to help your people. This cannot be done by word alone. You much be active with the individuals you work with and take the action that will show them you are there to help them obtain their dreams.

The old saying is true that people don't care how much you know until they know how much you care. Remember that you are trying to build individuals to be successful presidents of their own companies. By helping them and supporting them so as to be able to repeat their success, you are teaching them how to fish rather than just tossing them a fish. Your support can help them learn to help themselves and make a great catch in their network business. It is also important to focus on them as individuals and how each felt and what each thought about his performance. It is true that people gain more self-esteem and confidence by sharing their feelings with you than they ever will by just hearing your praise. Your listening reinforces your commitment to raise them to be successful in the business. By listening rather than talking you will let others discover themselves and what they need to do to be successful. Be high touch and listen to your people.

One of the most important aspects of high touch is helping individuals feel like they are part of the team and helping them discover a course that is worth pursuing. There is nothing worse than feeling lost, alone or uncertain about where you are going. It is vital to keep in mind that networking is working together and not a sporting event with set winners and losers. In networking everyone must win if the group is to win over the long-term. Again, build your people with praise and a sense of belonging. You don't have to squash others to succeed yourself. In fact, you must strengthen others if you want to really make it in the high touch world of networking.

John and Giselle:

We know that by creating an atmosphere of high touch you can really add value to another's life. The high tech aspect of the business should be used as a tool to give you more time for the high touch!

Marathoners
Vs
Sprinters

John and Giselle:

You will encounter all kinds of people as you build your network. Some will be looking for a quick buck, some will be looking for a career, and some will just be looking for a supplement to their income. Two out of the three are great for your network and will be a wonderful addition for you. The other usually creates problems and frustrations and in the end does more damage than good. We classify the two different types of people as Marathoners and Sprinters. As their names connote the Marathoners are those who can endure the long hard race of networking and Sprinters may do great over the short-run but generally fade quickly.

Lets take a look at the characteristics of these two types of individuals. The sprinter is only concerned with short-term profits and the marathoner is creating long-term relationships. The sprinter may use hard sell tactics and not be sensitive to the needs of his people. He is often offensive and may end up turning entire neighborhoods and communities away from the network. The Marathoner, on the other hand, knows that if he is to succeed he must have others around him who are loyal to the network and feel good about what they are doing and the contribution they are making.

The sprinter pushes specials and quotas where the marathoner moves quality product to end users. A lot of high pitch specials and incentives will only work over a limited period of time. People get tired of them and eventually are turned off. It is much like the carrot and the horse philosophy of motivation. The horse will keep moving as long as he is hungry and the carrot is appealing, but if he is full or doesn't see a bigger carrot coming, he will stop. The marathoner realizes that the motivation must be internal and tied to a sense of purpose and mission. He helps his network gain a better understanding of the product and the benefits it gives anyone who uses it. The marathoner also knows that by focusing on steady, gradual growth he can build individuals who will have the stamina to go the distance.

Sprinters go for any deal where marathoners search for win-win or no deal. The sprinter in his mad dash for cash will often compromise important principles and ethics which are vital to the long-term success of the organization. The marathoner assists every individual who is looking at the product and the business opportunity to evaluate all of the possibilities and make an informed and wise decision. You must operate on this premise: If they win, I win too. There is no other way to succeed in this business without a solid commitment to win-win.

Giselle:

Becoming a marathoner in this business is a very gratifying and rewarding experience. I will never forget the day at the beach club near our home having lunch with the children. The sun was shining and the view of the ocean outside the restaurant window was truly spectacular. As we ate, I overheard someone at the table behind me speaking Spanish. The voice sounded amazingly familiar. I turned around to find my childhood friend Marie who I hadn't seen for over 20 years. We were both shocked not only to meet again but to meet in a fancy place in an exclusive community in Florida. We laughed at the chance meeting and reminisced about our native Puerto Rico. We were a long way from the dusty streets of the middle class environment of San Juan. Marie asked, "What are you doing here?" She was amazed when I told her that I lived in the community and I pointed out my house to her. She said, "You married a millionaire! I am so happy for you!" She was even more surprised when I told her that I didn't marry a millionaire but that John and I had built our success and wealth together. We set up a dinner appointment so we could get our husbands together. Marie's husband, Fernando, is a well known celebrity who has several recording albums and has appeared in television shows and movies. As we ate, he asked about our business and was extremely impressed with the quality of our products and the opportunity in the business. Fernando said that he was so excited because this business gave him a chance to not only motivate and inspire people but actually give them a vehicle to live out their dreams. Both Fernando and Marie have joined the network and are moving things along. Being a marathoner in this business is thrilling. You will find that longevity in the business is one of your greatest assets. Take a moment right now and visualize yourself as a marathoner in this business. Picture yourself 20 years from now meeting an old friend. What kind of story are you going to be able to share with that friend? What kind of success and freedom will you be experiencing? Commit today to become a marathoner and enjoy the rewards that will surely follow.

John and Giselle:

We have seen many sprinters enter the business only to be a memory a few months down the road. We have also seen some wonderful marathoners who stick to solid principles and achieve success over many months and years. Remember, it is far better to be a rising star than a shooting star that quickly fades into oblivion.

The Leadership Challenge

John and Giselle:

Many of the topics we have discussed thus far in this book have a direct relationship to leadership. Your ability to lead yourself and others will determine your level of success in networking. We would like to discuss briefly how leadership qualities tie together and what you can do to improve your leadership skills.

First of all, we will establish that there are clearly two elements in the leadership equation. When most of us think of leadership we think of the company president, head coach or star athlete. This is one element of leadership - outward leadership. What many of us fail to look at is personal leadership - inward leadership. It is difficult at best to perform well as a leader of others until we are effective leaders of ourselves. Leadership is learned and not inborn. All of us have the ability to lead. We just have to search within ourselves to find and develop the qualities of leadership. Leadership is within each of us so that is where we need to begin looking for it. No one else can really teach you to be a leader. Others can point you in the direction leadership but you must teach yourself because the leader is already within you!

Personal leadership begins with the establishment of a personal mission or vision. This is where you identify who you are, what you stand for and how you go about fulfilling your mission. This is usually more a process of discovery than it is a process of creation. It is a process of discovering you. Write down all of the character traits you wish to possess as a leader and as a creator of wealth. Once you have achieved some success go back to your list and make sure that you are living in harmony with the values, character traits and mission you created. Far too many people abandone their values and mission once they being to succeed. One key aspect of purpose and personal mission is to make the commitment to do whatever is necessary to become a leader. Then you must commit to share your knowledge and leadership with others to empower them to become a leader. For us the business of networking helped us naturally discover what we truly wanted out of this life and what kind of contribution we were going to make. Remember that there are no accidental leaders. You have to develop your leadership abilities from within, starting with your mission. We have created a mission and purpose and are enjoying the journey, making our purpose a reality.

Once you have decided your purpose, you need to establish specific goals and objectives that can be written down, time framed and measured. If you cannot write out your goal, put a date or time when you will complete it and be able to check and monitor your progress along the way, the goal is too general or vague. Remember once again that when we deal in generalities, we very rarely succeed; but when we deal in specifics, we very rarely fail. Your journey to success can begin right now with you and a blank sheet of paper. Take some time and write down in specific detail what you want to accomplish and the action plan that will lead you there.

Developing self-discipline is vital to personal leadership. You must have the ability to stick to your goals long after the mood in which you created them has passed. It is easy to set a goal, it is a challenge to see it through to the end. Self-discipline gives you the courage and energy to continue pursuing your goals and dreams even when things don't look so good or feel so good. Self discipline also will help you get out of your comfort zones and aid you in attacking challenges head on. Discipline will help you become a better you and a better leader. This aspect of personal leadership can and will allow you to enjoy the fruits of networking.

You must be able to control your time and your priorities. If you are in a reactive mode to the external forces of life, you will never be able to accomplish anything worth while. Establishing daily and weekly priorities will keep you focused on things that matter most. Remember that activity alone does not equal production or accomplishment. You have to be able to not only do things right but you must be sure that you are doing the right things.

Personal leadership also demands that you have a good balance in your life. Pursuing a goal at the expense of family, friends or your health is a journey to destruction. You must take the time to create health if you are going to enjoy wealth. No sum of money can be enjoyed or shared without your health. It takes just a little extra time to eat right and exercise, but the energy and esteem you will feel as a result will help you succeed in every aspect of your life.

Achieving a balance also requires that you take the time to smell the roses and deepen your ties with others. It has often been said that life is like a wheel and in order to enjoy it to the fullest you must keep your wheel in balance with all kinds of different activities.

Once you have solidified your ability to lead yourself, you can then become an effective leader of others. Leading other people does not require you to be an eloquent speaker, a charismatic conversationalist or a General MacArthur. There are a few characteristics and skills that effective leaders possess and all of them can be learned.

A dynamic leader has a deep commitment to a cause. This is why you have to begin with personal leadership. You must establish that cause or mission and then be able to share it with others. Again this doesn't have to be done with words alone. In fact, it is more effectively done by action.

Example is by far the most powerful arrow in your leadership quiver. You can talk to them until you are blue in the face, but your actions speak volumes about who you are and what your mission is. The people in your network will be watching every move you make and imitating and emulating what you do. Always present yourself in the best possible way in all situations because with networking, everyone you meet could possibly become a member of your team.

Leaders are committed to helping others. You must have a deep and firm commitment to each individual in your organization. Express that feeling by word, action and deed. Appreciate in advance, like we have discussed, and let your people know that your commitment to them is unconditional. You will be there for them at every turn regardless of whether they are producing big numbers or small.

Teamwork is crucial to a successful network. As the leader of your network you must develop a strong sense of belonging for every member of your team. This is another aspect of effective leadership. True leaders help every team member feel like they are part of the championship effort. There are no small roles or positions on winning teams. Your ability to create this feeling within your network team will determine your long term success in the business. Remember, again that you are really paid for your leadership. When you invest in leadership you are investing in yourself.

A strong attribute of leaders is the ability to create a sense of positive urgency and importance to their cause. They do this by sharing all aspects of the cause and what will happen with action or no action. They are able to help others understand and support their mission. They often do this with their example of high energy action and productivity. If you see someone working their heart out, you will tend to feel a sense of urgency about their cause and will most likely join in and assist them in their effort. Effective leaders create this positive energy by using impending events. If a person feels that an impending event is important, exciting and will add value to their lives they will come in a hurry. Positive urgency also helps to establish a sense of belonging. If your people feel the urgency of your message they will also feel that they are a vital cog in the wheel. This will solidify their commitment and further the effectiveness of your network. Create a sense of positive urgency within your network for the great cause at hand which is a cause that will enable everyone in your network to thrive and succeed. Urgency sends a message of take action now so you can achieve now and enjoy the fruit of your labors. Lead your people with a sense of positive urgency.

The positive urgency for my network cause came as a result of a walk in the park. It was a beautiful summer day. At the time I was still running my manufacturing company and things were very hectic. I walked out the door holding the hands of Jonathan and Natalie, my children. We walked for a while and I don't remember much of what I saw or where we were headed when a sharp pull brought me to reality. Jonathan was tugging on my arm and shouting, "Dad, can't you hear me? Dad, are you paying attention?" I quickly checked my watch to find that we had been gone for almost 20 minutes! I had been so totally consumed by my work at the office that I hadn't heard a word my children said for our entire walk. Urgency came in with a rush. If I couldn't be with my children even when I was with my children, I needed a change! I needed the freedom to not only be with them physically but truly be there and become a part of their lives. This urgency to have the freedom to spend time with my family and enjoy life to the fullest has been a driving force in my own quest for leadership.

Leaders empower others to achieve instead of dictating every move. As a leader your goal should be to help people become leaders themselves. Too many leaders want to manage their people rather than lead them. Too many leaders try to control their people and hold on to all of the power themselves. This is like getting a drink of water with your hands; if you try to squeeze, hold and control the water, it will run through your fingers. But, if you cup your hand gently you can enjoy a refreshing drink. With your people you need to let go and share every bit of knowledge you gain with them as soon as possible. True leaders empower their people with knowledge and insight.

If you do everything for your people all the time and tell them how and why to do everything, they develop what is called learned helplessness. They become dependent on you to do and initiate everything. This may feel good to your ego but it won't allow you to capitalize on the multiplication factor. If you are doing everyone's job and spending time dictating your distributor's actions, you will actually be running on a negative multiplication factor. You will not only diminish their effectiveness but you will take your own down to zero. Effective leaders communicate what needs to be done, then they empower their people to create the best methods for the accomplishment of the goal. Don't tell your people what to do or how to do everything. Give them the necessary knowledge that will allow them to do it for themselves. This requires a great deal of trust and belief in the abilities of your people. If you show them that you trust them and that you are confident that they can create good results, they will quickly develop into leaders themselves. True leaders build leaders.

Leaders are great at adapting to change. In order to succeed at anything in life you must be able to adapt and change. Every coach knows his game plan before the first whistle blows, yet rarely, if ever, is that game plan in the same form when the game ends. Successful coaches have to adapt and adjust to the changing circumstances around them. As the leader of your business you must be able to do the same. You have to adapt to different people, circumstances and belief systems. You must be constantly changing and updating your game plan for success. The computer business is another great example of managing change. Can you imagine what this world would be like if everyone had been satisfied with the computers of just a few years ago? The computers of that day were amazing, but now they are only a shadow of all that can be done. The leaders in the computer industry promoting constant change have allowed it to thrive and grow geometrically over the last 10 years. You cannot run your business on the philosophies or practices of 10 years ago. You may try but you will stagnate and be unproductive. You cannot win this year's Superbowl on last year's game plan. You must guide your people along the path of change and make sure that they see change as a positive step toward a better future. Don't become a fat cat who sits back thinking they have done everything and can rest on their laurels. You will either be green and growing or ripe and rotting. It is true that there is only one constant in life and that is change! Use it to achieve your dreams.

Leadership equals knowledge. Knowledge is a driving force for consistent growth in your network and in yourself as a leader. The more knowledge you acquire, the stronger you will become. You will be in a position to take on even the most difficult challenge with a wide array of knowledge and experience. True leaders are always searching for and penetrating the outer limits of knowledge and understanding.

Leaders are forever learning. At one of the company conventions Giselle ran up to Craig B. to thank him for all that he had taught us and for all the help that he had delivered. She expected him to say something like; "It was nothing" or possibly "Your welcome." Instead, he replied "We all learn from each other. Thank you, for what you have taught me." Here was the leader of the company thanking Giselle and me! I have learned that there is much to be learned from everyone in this business regardless of their experience or personal success. The key is to have an open mind and be willing to listen and learn. Some of the greatest things I have learned have come from the most unexpected sources. If you are not coachable or teachable in networking you will never develop into a high performance leader.

True leaders can turn an adversity into an opportunity for growth and achievement. Help your people to overcome any problems they might encounter, from rejection to dream stealers and everything in between. You are there to guide them through the tough times and assist them in achieving their best.

It is often said that leadership is an art. We believe that it is an art and a science. Most, if not all, of the key elements of leadership are directly within your control and they can be learned and developed. Again, knowledge is a vital element. A natural by-product of applied knowledge is consistent growth. Use your knowledge as a powerful leadership tool. In addition to your gaining leadership by attaining more knowledge, you must remember the one overridding leadership stipulation is that you must earn it. It is not something that is bestowed upon you, nor is it an entitlement received automatically because of your position. There really isn't a way to leadership; leadership is the way! Every experience you have will empower you to be a better leader. Being a leader is the full expression of who you really are. Leadership is really synonymous with becoming You! So begin today by building a better you and then go out and share all that you have, gain the respect of others, and become a dynamic leader of your network.

Putting it all Together

John and Giselle:

We have talked about a lot of different aspects of networking and many of the key habits and attitudes required to succeed. Now we would like to walk you through the process itself and help you put it all together.

For us, the first step was finding the right company. Having the right company is critical to your success. There are many networking companies out there that are not committed to long-term success. As you evaluate networking companies make sure that you don't look for magic, but search for excellence. We found excellence with our parent company and are thrilled at their addition of a second division. Our company is based on the highest moral and ethical standards. They have products that have been tested and proven over time. They have a total commitment to quality in every aspect of the business. They also have an unwavering commitment to every distributor and retail customer. They have shown us time and time again of their allegiance to our success. Support is quick, timely and always professional. Promises made are promises kept.

As you look into networking make sure that you check to see that the company is consumer protective. Be certain that they are committed to taking quality products to and end consumer. Also research and discover if distributors are actually being paid. Ask others if they are truly receiving the compensation as outlined in the distributor agreement. It is also worth the time to contact several distributors to see if the parent company has changed the compensation plan. We have seen too many networking companies that continually change the compensation plan and literally rob the distributors of their rewards. It is like someone changing the finish line in a race over and over again. Just when you think you can cross the line and enjoy the fruits of success they back it up and make you meet new criteria. Be very selective in choosing your networking company. A good company will pay you for your efforts and will continually introduce new, state-of-the-art products that meet the needs and wants of consumers. Create a list of criteria for a networking company that meets your needs and has the same value and ethics that you have.

The actions and efforts of your network headquarters should never cause you to doubt their intent or purpose. If you do, then you may be working in the wrong network. Loyalty is the name of the game.

We have found that there are three major confidences that must be established before anyone can succeed in networking. First you must have total confidence in the parenting company. Again, for us this was easy based on the actions of our parent company and their incredible commitment to the long-term success of each distributor and to quality products. Product is what drives the business and must be a focus of the highest priority. The products we represent are, without a doubt, the highest quality in the world. You must use the products on a regular basis and experience their effectiveness for yourself.

The second confidence is that you will have an opportunity to receive a great return on the investment of your time and energy over the long-term. This confidence gives you the ability to totally throw yourself into your business. If you don't think you will get a good return, you will always be hesitant about putting in the necessary time to succeed. With our parent company we knew without a doubt that our return on invested time would outshine anything in the world. Examine the compensation plan very closely to see if the organization is really committed to the distributors. Do they really pay for your ability to lead others and help them succeed? Do they pay for your ability to support the people in your network? Does the compensation plan give you a vested interest in leading and supporting individuals throughout the network? The compensation plan will dictate the kind of culture that will develop in your organization so look at it closely and make sure that they are committing generous compensation to the network. Finally, you must gain confidence in yourself. The only way you can do this is by being productive and getting out in the real world and making things happen. Success truly breeds more success, enthusiasm breeds enthusiasm and confidence breeds more confidence.

You have two kinds of assets as you begin your networking business; tangible and intangible. The parent company possesses most of the tangibles. They are things like product and packaging. You have tangibles such as a telephone. The intangibles that you possess are the essence of the second two confidences described above. It is an asset to know that you will be rewarded for your efforts and that you will receive a return on your investment of self. Also to know that you can do it is perhaps the most important asset any of us possess. The combination of these tangible and intangible assets will put you on a track to incredible achievement.

Remember that wealth is not found, nor is it static, nor is it based on resources. Natural resources do not ensure wealth nor do they prevent wealth. Japan has few natural resources but they have developed into one of the wealthiest and most productive countries in the world. Wealth truly is a natural by-product of productivity. There is no money in knowledge alone. You have to apply it or share it if you want to enjoy any of its value. The freedom to pursue self-interest creates wealth and allows you to discover the real you. It is also true that if you are allowed to pursue self-interests you can create not only wealth but the freedom to enjoy it. Remember that this is self-interest and not selfish-interest. It is truly the freedom to serve others, make a bigger contribution to family, friends and society and a ticket to experience all that life has to offer.

Having made a commitment to networking, your next challenge is to create a mission and a game plan for your involvement. Many people start out part-time in this business and that is great. The key is to make sure that you stick to your plan and to also remember that part-time does not mean spare-time. If you commit to working ten hours a week to start, then do it every single week. Don't let there be any exceptions! Be aware of the villain of procrastination and don't let it carry out the assassination of your motivation. Keep focused and on track and you will be able to truly extend yourself and your abilities through your network.

We guarantee that as soon as you make a commitment to networking, that the dream stealers will come out in full force. They will hit you at every turn and try to pull you off of your track to success and freedom. Even the people you love the most may try to steal your dream. Be sure to stay focused on the desired results you are pursuing and don't look back!

Know your products. You must have a firm belief in your products and literally be a product of your product if you want to succeed. Again, for us this was easy because our products are some of the finest and most effective in the world. They truly make a difference in the way you live and the way you feel about yourself. It is very easy for us to get excited about our products because we have seen the difference in our own lives.

Make your contacts and pursue them with all your might. Many of your best people will enter only after you have shown them what a strong commitment you have and how much you want them to succeed in the business. Be patient and not too pushy. Everything comes in good time. You don't have to force a do or die decision on anyone. Show them the benefits and let them make a good decision for themselves. Remember also that timing is very important in this business. Not everyone is ready to make the same commitment or effort that you are making right now. Give them time, be enthusiastic, be committed and lead by example.

Get your family involved in what you are doing. We have thoroughly enjoyed having our five children be very much involved in our business. It will help them develop great habits and attitudes and also an appreciation for the effort it takes to live a wonderful lifestyle. It is also important to remember that is no value or joy if you arrive at success without the ones you love.

Organize your time and your priorities. Be certain that your activities lead to accomplishment and not just to more activities. You must be focused on producing desired results. Keep score and see where you are in relationship to your higher goals and dreams. Evaluate this on a daily and weekly basis.

Work to give just a little bit more. It is true that in most things in life that the little things make a big difference. In the Olympics it always comes down to a hundredth of a point, a fraction of a second, or the width of tire that is the difference in becoming a gold medal winner or an also ran. As we have shown throughout this book, by just adding a little bit to your efforts, the synergy and multiplying effect of the network can create amazing results. Focus on doing the little things that will take you to the top of the mountain of success and personal freedom.

Have fun! This business is about having fun. If you are not enjoying the journey you will be disappointed when you arrive. You have a wonderful opportunity in networking to create friendships and relationships that will become far superior to the business itself. Laugh at your mistakes and blunders and enjoy the medicine of a good laugh.

Once you have committed to these simple principles you must make a firm resolve to complete four stages of training and development. These stages are vital for your success in the business, which also means that you need to take everyone you sponsor into the business through the exact same process. First you must go through what we call "doing your homework" which includes: using the product, reading and studying information about the business, creating a list of people in your circle of influence and possibly visiting the home office. This is your "due diligence" phase. I always tell people to not take my word, but to find out for themselves. The second phase is called initial training. In this phase you continue to use the product, ask questions about the business, evaluate your circle of influence to see who would be best to start with, establish your commitment level, create six month and one year goals, commit to how many hours you will work each week, place your initial order to obtain supplies and samples based on your commitment and goals, learn how to approach people, create interest, set appointments, give effective presentations and close (help people get what they want by making wise and informed decisions.) The third phase of training is called basic training. This covers the first thirty days in the business. You should work closely with others in your network to obtain support and feedback on what you are doing and what you need to accomplish to move to the next level in the business. This is where you begin to develop leadership, both in yourself and in those you sponsor. Keep in close contact and monitor and be monitored so you can improve your performance. This is a time to constantly review what you learned in the initial training and expand your abilities in each area of the initial training. The fourth phase is what we call coaching for success. This phase covers the first ninety days in the business and is a time of improvement, correction and solidification. This is where you can really ignite the after burners and truly duplicate yourself. In the fourth stage you will learn what being productive is all about. You will learn that just selling a product does not necessarily mean you are productive. You are productive only if you have a satisfied customer. You are not effective when you sponsor someone new into the business. You are effective only if that person is trained and they are able to become effective themselves. This requires total commitment and focus and is an exciting time of growth and achievement. There are many supplements to this book that can help you successfully accelerate and complete these four stages of training and development. **Please feel free to call Innovative Learning Technologies for further information, support and materials for training.**

We have truly learned that it is impossible to achieve excellence alone. It is also difficult to attain financial freedom based on your own singular effort. You must leverage yourself and your abilities with the help of others. You must extend yourself and expand your influence to greater numbers if you are to truly experience success and fulfillment. The greatest joy comes when you reach your full potential, become the best you can be and live in harmony with your values.

We sincerely believe that everyone can achieve and experience success at the highest levels. As we look at those individuals who have found success in networking we see that there is no set pattern to background, age or experience. Seniors as well as young people, white collar and blue collar, educated and uneducated have all made it in this business. The common thread among this diverse group of individuals is hard work and a willingness to pay the price of success. Is it easy? NO! Is it worth it? YES!

We hope that you have enjoyed this little journey into the realms of successful networking. We have encountered an abundance of wealth, happiness and enjoyment over the past seven years that has been breathtaking and exciting. We assure you that the same outcome is there for you through Networking... The Natural Extension of You! Good luck! John and Giselle will be looking for you on the beaches of the world...

All inquiries for additional information, materials, training and quantity discount prices should be directed to Innovative Learning Technologies, 8184 Highland Dr., Sandy, Utah 84093, 1-800-934-8946.